Biograph

Christie Spurling was born on the 7th May 1975. He was immediately put into care and spent the first few months of his life in a children's home. He was one of the lucky ones and was adopted. Christie has had a rollercoaster ride of a life so far, with times of great challenge. He now runs N-Gage, a Manchester-based youth charity. He is married to Jo and has two daughters. Outside work Christie is a keen drummer and petrol-head.

Endorsements

"I have known Christie for a long time and have seen first-hand how he has overcome challenges in his own life to reach out to young people with amazing results!"

Debra Green OBE, Founder and National Director ROC

"The way Christie has used his past life experiences to develop the charity N-Gage is inspiring".

Kevin Kennedy, actor and former Coronation Street star and wife Clare CEO, Cornerstone Recovery

"This is the story of an exceptional young man who, through his faith, turned his life around, and in so doing brought hope and opportunity to many disaffected young people of Manchester. His charity N-Gage is an inspiration to all. A life turned around to the benefit of others - much can be learned by many from Christie's story".

Christine Druce, Social Worker who placed Christie in his family

"What an adventure! Christie's story from 'rescued' to 'rescuer' is both inspiring and transformational".

Anthony Delaney, Leader of Ivy Churches, Manchester, and former Police Officer

"Christie is an example of a life transformed; now transforming lives through the work of N-Gage. Not only have Christie and his wife, Jo, taken huge leaps of faith that have allowed N-Gage to develop as it has, their daily walk of faith enables it to continue bringing hope to desperate situations and showing love to the overlooked in society. In part, N-Gage achieves what it does through the authenticity of Christie and his colleagues, and through its development and delivery of credible and effective programmes".

Dr Hayley Entwistle, Clinical Psychologist

"Christie's book has inspired me in many ways: he is a prime example that with God's guidance anything is possible; this book laminates this through Christie's story. He has inspired me to work with young people to be a positive role model in their lives like he has been in mine".

Jade Bogle, young person who has benefitted from the work of N-Gage

"This book is really inspiring: not only does it help the reader to understand why children might be behaving in a certain manner, it also reminds us of our part to play in the healing process for children who have had such difficult starts to their lives. As a school leader the work that Christie and the N-Gage team have undertaken to change children's lives reminds me of the reasons why I became a headteacher. This book shows us that the journey may be a challenge, but inspirational people can help us on our way".

Sarah Rudd, Headteacher, Newall Green Primary School

"Christie, not only are you a true man, you're a gent. We don't deal with disappointment, pain, hurt etc. by either giving in, or by burying it. We get messy; we fight; we accept our vulnerability. Sometimes we accept we're lost and need to look at the map - and preferably get a bit rude and stubborn on the way (that's my interpretation anyway). Whatever it takes to keep walking the path that He leads us on, full in the knowledge that His love is immense for us, but the journey is not easy".

Dave Reynolds, family friend

"This book is the Jam! Not only is it real to the reader, it also takes us on a journey into the lives of so many disaffected young people! As I see thousands of hurting young people face to face, a book like this reminds me of why I do what I do and inspires me to be better at it! The N-Gage team are heroes!"

Lindz West, Frontman LZ7 and CEO of Light

FACING MY PAST
UNLOCKING THE
FUTURE

CHRISTIE SPURLING

ISBN: 978-0-9927271-2-3

Design & typesetting by Mike Thorpe, Design Chapel Ltd www.design-chapel.com

Printed and bound by UAB "Spindulio spaustuve"

Vakarinis aplinkkelis 24, LT-48184 Kaunas, Lithuania

Acknowledgments

Ems Hancock, for reading this book bit by bit and helping make sense of my thoughts.

John Hancock, who was really encouraging and helped me feel confident to proceed as I first began pondering writing my book.

Anthony Delaney, for writing the foreword. You never know what to expect when you ask someone to write about you. Anthony's kind words touched both Jo and me.

Mike Thorpe, for the graphic design of the book and cover design
www.design-chapel.com

Lucy Smith, from Smith Imaging, for the cover photo
www.smithimaging.co.uk

Andy Smith for his front cover design.

My proof readers: Ann Hancock, Helena Monck, Simon Chesterson and Catherine Milsom.

My endorsees: Debra Green, Kevin and Clare Kennedy, Lindz West, Christine Druce, Anthony Delaney, Hayley Entwistle, Jade Bogle, Sarah Rudd and Dave Reynolds.

I would like to thank all the staff and trustees, past and present, for the amazing support you have offered me to help make N-Gage the success it has become.

Thanks also to Lymm Baptist Church and Ivy Church Manchester for all their support over the years and to my church leaders past and present including Frank and Debra Green, Graham and Anne Derbyshire, Brian and Chris Howden, Anthony and Zoe Delaney, Selwyn and Helen White and many others.

Finally, I'd also like to thank all the youth workers and teachers who have helped me over the years.

Dedication

I would like to dedicate this book to my wife Jo and daughters Amy and Ella for inspiring me to be the best person I can be. I'd also like to dedicate this to Dad and Mum for giving me the chance to have a life which has been far better because they adopted me. To my brother and sisters for all you have done for me over the years. Finally to all those who have invested in me over the past forty years through the good times and bad.

Contents

Foreword

We all love stories. We are used to hearing them from being a child. Perhaps you sat on a parent's knee as the wonder began, *'Once upon a time'*. There was a beginning, a middle and an end where all *'lived happily ever after'*.

But now we have grown we know that's not everybody's story. Some people have a struggle, a journey and a fight; many despair that they may never reach that *'happily ever after'*, not in this life anyway.

I have known Christie Spurling and his family as close friends for over six years. During that time I've seen him grow and emerge in life as he has courageously come to terms with parts of his story that he knew about already, and other chapters which were a surprise and even a shock to him, and they will move you as you read it here.

We don't get to choose our story, our only choice perhaps is that in the role we get to play: will we be a victim or like Christie, step up, scarred yet unbowed, as a hero? That word is used too lightly these days, but I do not hesitate to say that this man is and has continued to be something of a hero to me and many others - especially young people looking for someone in the face of their own adversity, confusion and challenges. He continues to go forward with hope, faith and love into the future and enables them to do so too.

I have been privileged to go into a tough inner city school in Manchester with Christie where a group of well-behaved young people have engaged with him so well that I left thinking they must be the best and brightest in the school. 'You should have seen them six weeks ago,' Christie smiles, as he tells me some of their stories. Young people at risk of exclusion, given one last chance – and fortunate that Christie was that chance.

Christie has found himself perfectly positioned to be able to bring comfort, empathy and a bigger dream to a disillusioned, hurting and lost generation, through his award-winning work with N-Gage. Christie's life experience connects to their hearts and his story will, I'm sure, encourage and inspire you as it has so many so far. This is a story that needs to be told and needs to be heard by our nation, and I'm sure that when you have read it you will want to pass it on to others.

This book is a kind of memoir or autobiography. Its tough *'Once upon a time'* beginning opens up a thrilling adventure and a great number of love stories in the middle. I am fully confident that this story will encourage you in your story, and will turn out very, very well in the end.

Reverend Anthony Delaney

Leader of Ivy Churches, Manchester, and former Police Officer

CHAPTER 1

In the beginning

---

*"You saw me before I was born. Every day of my
life was recorded in your book. Every moment was
laid out before a single day had passed."*

Psalm 139:16

Chosen

My adoptive mum, Jan, told me how my story began:

She worked in a village where Dr Barnardo had lived and set up a children's village. Whilst her work was rewarding, she was distressed that so many children, especially those who were black or disabled, were never placed in families for adoption. Many weekends saw her taking little ones back to her house to give them a break from the children's home and a taste of normal family life. Mum and Dad discussed adoption before they got married. They agreed they wanted four children and decided that if they were blessed with two of their own, they would adopt two. They also agreed that if they adopted one black child they would also adopt another so there would be support in the family.

At this time, placing black children into white families wasn't something that was 'done'. Still today the issue of 'transracial' adoption is hugely controversial, with experts divided on what is best for the young, vulnerable children.

The social worker that Jan and Rodger were assigned to was an amazing woman called Chris Druce who worked for Rotherham Social Services. She was incredibly supportive of what they were trying to do and helped them in every way she could. Chris and Mum went on to become good friends and they still are in contact with each other. (I still get a Christmas card from Chris each year, usually with some encouraging words about my work and how my life has panned out).

At this time, I was an 8-month-old baby and living in a children's home in Portsmouth. Because Mum and Dad lived in Sheffield it wasn't possible to arrange visits to Portsmouth so it was agreed that, after staying in Chelmsford for Christmas, they would travel down to Portsmouth to collect me with Nikki and Jo, who were to become my new sisters, and my brother Toby. They fed me lunch and packed up what belongings I had and took me home. It was a long journey and no one could get me to smile!

In the mid-70s introductions and visits to children were not a part of the procedure for adoption. There was a lot of discussion with Chris Druce and lots of prayer too. Of course, this was more than a life-changing decision for me. I was chosen. I was rescued. But my life was still not going to be easy. Nor was it going to be easy for the family that I was adopted into.

Attachment Disorder

Apparently when my new parents came to collect me I was in a big room on my own. This was a picture of how I must have been feeling. Because I was being looked after by lots of different people, I never got the opportunity to bond with one consistent care-giver. Even though I was still a baby I had developed an attachment disorder. In later life this was to prove a stumbling block to building any kind of meaningful relationship.

The Mayo Clinic describes Attachment Disorder (which begins usually during the first 6-12 months) as having the following symptoms in babies:

- Withdrawn, sad and listless appearance

- Failure to smile

- Lack of the normal tendency to follow others in the room with the eyes

- Failure to reach out when picked up

- No interest in playing interactive games

- No interest in playing with toys

- Calm when left alone

- Screaming a lot

My parents tell me that I rarely cried or smiled.

Early years

Once adopted, they changed my name from Darren Allen to Christie Darren. They chose Christie because I was adopted at Christmas. I often joked that I was glad they didn't adopt me at Easter because I would have hated being called Easter Bunny!

After the adoption was finalised I lived in Sheffield for the first few years of life as a Spurling. I am told that even at that early stage I was a cause for concern. Mum tells me she felt sad that I had had such a difficult start in life. Mum and Dad had two children of their own; my sisters Joanne and Nicola. Around this time they also adopted my brother, Toby. My brother was in the same situation as me, being a black child in a white family. Looking back, it was good that it worked out this way as we could share the experience together. There was no doubt that we stood out like two 'sore thumbs', but we had a loving family and we were very lucky to be in that position.

I have memories of that Sheffield house and can vaguely remember the road we lived on. I also vaguely remember my oldest sister being chased by a dog and being bitten. In 1976 I was taken for dedication at church. Little did people realise what that symbolic act would go on to mean for me later in life.

We were all taken to church every Sunday and took part in Sunday school. Dad was heavily involved in the leadership of the church and has been ever since in the various churches we attended over the years. I often wonder if he would have ended up in full time Christian leadership if things had been different in the earlier years of my life.

It quickly became apparent that my adoption into the family was not necessarily going to be easy for all concerned. I can't remember a huge amount about that time, but I had become untrusting and did not want to let people get too close to me. As you will hear throughout this story, there were times when the attachment disorder was like a crippling disease, limiting my ability to develop like a normal child and stopping me from forming meaningful relationships. Even now, traces of it still linger in me. As I have grown older, I have learnt to cope with it better.

We lived in Sheffield for a while longer; I continued to be a cause for concern, becoming more withdrawn and outwardly unhappy. Aged three we moved due to Dad's work. Dad worked as a sales representative for a stationery company. He was relocated to Manchester so we settled in a very nice Cheshire village called Lymm. For me, life continued in much the same vein. I started nursery and hated it. Being left there was awful for me. I wonder now if it was too similar an environment to the children's home; lots of people coming and going and too many kids in one room.

I carried on exhibiting challenging and worrying tendencies and behaviour. Now that I was being required to mix more and be around other children and adults who I did not know well, my attachment issues became even more obvious.e.

To have been adopted into a loving family and ending up living in a village like Lymm was such a blessing. But instead of recognising and living in the light of this, my game plan involved drawing as much negative attention to myself as possible. More about this as my story progresses!

Primary school years and tears

I moved from nursery into primary school and became even more of a handful. By this stage I could be very moody and stubborn. Even then the amount of time I took up from the teacher compared to the other 29 pupils was high. I was useless at playing with other children and hated being in a big group. I would only put effort into things I could be bothered doing. As I grew up, I spent more and more of my time winding other pupils up and stopping them working. As these were the days before classes had teaching assistants I know that my behaviour must have had a huge impact on others' ability to learn.

Things continued on a downward spiral. Among my peers I was tolerated and used as a way of getting laughs, but I never really felt I had any 'best mates'. I found it easier being around adults and did form some good relationships with a handful of teachers. I continued to be a challenge in primary school and right up to leaving for secondary school I was constantly in trouble.

There were things I was good at, like running and music. I could do the 100 metres sprint and hurdles faster than pretty much anyone in my year and was really encouraged to pursue this. It was a talent that came in very handy when I was running away from local teenagers who I had a habit of winding up!

It was also in primary school that I got into drumming. I had a natural sense of rhythm and was really pushed to do drumming. If I had a rare week when I was really good I was allowed to take home a snare drum and stand to practice on. If I was 'bad' and not allowed, I would wait till no one was home and play on my Mum's pans with wooden spoons. I was quickly asked to play in the school orchestra and this was used as an incentive to try and get me to behave. My behaviour was still a real cause for concern as I was often very withdrawn and unwilling to mix with others. I would avoid playing with people at school and it really became apparent to me at this age that I preferred my own company and I would spend hours in my room on my own. I liked reading and would do this for hours on end.

Standing out

As I went through primary school I started spending more and more time outside the Head's office. In fact, it got to the point in the end where they placed a fold-down table for me behind the Head's door. It was left there for me to use on the frequent occasions I was thrown out of class.

By now, aged about seven, I was developing an explosive temper and would take people by surprise when I erupted. I also used to storm out of class a lot as I knew I would end up being sent out of most lessons. I was very easily led and would do stupid things people told me to do for a laugh. I was desperately trying to feel accepted and part of a group.

In the village we lived in there were only four other black children. One lived in the local children's home, one was my brother and one was another lad down the road who, like us, had been placed in a white family. We stood out in what was a very white, middle class, area. School photographs show

I was one of only a couple of black children in my class.

Daredevil

Being naïve and wanting to fit in, meant that even at this early age I was getting into all kinds of scrapes. I remember some older lads at primary school saying, "If you wee in the sink in the boys' toilets, we'll buy you ten gobstoppers after school."

I would do anything for gobstoppers (including stealing them), so I took up the challenge and did the deed. Just as I was finishing, the Head marched in with two of my challengers who were grinning from ear to ear. He asked me what I had just done and I explained, somewhat sheepishly, about the challenge. The other pupils rapidly disappeared. The Head stormed towards me and slapped me across the face! He told me never to dare do anything like that again. Unsurprisingly, I spent the rest of the week outside his office.

Incidentally, when I went home and explained that the Head had slapped me across the face, I half-expected some sympathy. I hoped I would be put in the car, my Dad driving me to the school at top speed to burst into the Head's office and slap him back, like a reckless superhero. Dad's response was far from it, "You must have done something to deserve it." he said, simply. "Let that be a lesson to you."

Imagine what would happen if a Headteacher slapped a pupil today! Although I am not advocating a return to smacking children, it taught me a lesson and I have, as far as I am aware, resisted the urge to urinate in sinks ever since!

I think because other pupils realised I was a bit of a daredevil they would challenge me to do stupid things and I would always oblige. As this became part of the way I operated, in and out of school, people used me to have fun, enjoying watching me get into trouble. It was a way for me to feel accepted by my peers, but it resulted in a childhood of consistently being in trouble.

I went through primary school continuing to exhibit even more challenging behaviour. As I got older, I got into many fights. My anger and rage terrified even me at times. I never really did well academically at primary school and although I was good at English, other subjects were a real struggle.

Most people assumed I was being lazy. I really struggled with maths and in later life discovered I had a logic disorder that stopped me being able to learn patterns of numbers. I also found out that I had Dyscalculia, which meant it was almost impossible for me to understand numbers, learn how to use them, or learn any facts relating to them. Even now I can't do basic maths sums and really struggle putting things into logical patterns.

Finding out my story

As my behaviour worsened at school I also became more aggressive at home. I argued a lot, rarely did as I was told and was very moody for my age. Sadly, my mum got the lion's share of my attitude problems. I think I struggled a great deal with the issues around my adoption. I could not understand the concept of a mother giving away a child. At this stage, I still did not know why I had been put in a children's home and I took this out on the mother figure in my life. At times, my bad behaviour towards my mum was terrible. Perhaps some of it was the usual growing up stuff all children go through but in my case this was magnified by those unanswered questions and resentments. My attitude towards Mum was frequently aggressive and at times I even told her I hated her; something I deeply regret now. I think adoptive mums are sometimes more of a target for hurt than adoptive fathers. A child sees a mother 'giving them up' as the ultimate rejection. For me, this emotional pain was definitely something I projected onto my adoptive mum, sometimes unintentionally.

Growing family

Soon Mum and Dad started fostering more children. Over a few years we had several children who came to stay for short, medium or long term periods. I often wonder what drove them to take on more children given the challenges I was presenting, as well as all the other pressures of family life. They were amazing! Looking back, it was good for us all as it gave us something (other than my poor behaviour) to focus on. Strangely, I enjoyed having the foster kids around too. Secretly I used to boast to others that my parents fostered children. It shows me now that I was proud and grateful for their selflessness towards myself, and others.

It wasn't always easy, however. I remember one time Dad had been on the motorway travelling back from a meeting and a dog had run out in front of him. He had a clear and nasty choice: hit the dog or cause a pile up. So the dog was hit. Dad was obviously very shaken by this and his company car was a bit of a mess. When he got home he walked in looking drained and shocked. As he came into the living room he was confronted with brand new 14 month old twins he had never seen before. Mum had had a call asking her to take them as an emergency placement and had been unable to get hold of Dad so had said yes, in his absence. Poor Dad had to recover quickly!

Why I was adopted

When I first started having thoughts about writing this book I decided I would be as honest as possible and try to share as much as I was comfortable with. I have since learnt that the way I was conceived is a vital, if ugly, part of my story. The pain of this has been something that has lingered in my life for many years. It explains some of the anger and aggression that I displayed as I moved through my childhood. It also made sense of some of the strange things I found myself doing as a child and as a teenager.

It is not something that I talk about a lot in my daily life. I am constantly aware of it and sometimes find it very upsetting to think about. But I understand now how overcoming it has helped me become who I am. Seeing the bigger picture like this has helped me start to deal with my past in a more positive way, hence the title of this book.

Being told

I suspect that one of the hardest things any adoptive parent has to cope with is knowing potentially horrifying details about a child you have taken as your own. Knowing that you will one day have to share those deeply unpleasant things with them must be such a burden. As you grow to love and accept this child as your own, I guess it must get even harder. I have often wondered what I would do if I was faced with the same situation and how I would work out when was the 'right time'. I think the simple answer is there is never such a time. Speaking from my own experience, I don't feel that it would have benefitted myself, or my family, for my mum and dad to have kept it from me any longer. They needed to let me know why I was behaving the way I was.

You may have heard the statement "if a child is born in love they learn to love, if a child is born in hate and aggression they learn to hate and be aggressive."

Just before I became a teenager my mum sat me down on the sofa and said there was something she needed to tell me. I don't know if something I had done on a bus a few days earlier had made her suddenly decide to tell me now.

We had been on a bus going to Warrington, our nearest big town. A black lady came and sat next to me. I remember getting up out of my seat and moving to another seat so I could sit alone. Due to being rejected at birth, I never felt comfortable around black women. Living in such a predominantly white area meant I didn't have to face my fears that often and on this day, I just couldn't handle it. This wasn't because I was racist, but because I was so fragile and hurt emotionally.

After this, Mum and Dad must have decided that now was the time to tell me about my history.

The truth

My real mother was raped. This was the reason she had decided to give me up as soon as I was born. I remember feeling shocked that I had been conceived in this way. Given my age, I think Mum did a great job of telling me this information. At that stage it utterly compounded all my feelings of rejection. For some time after that I truly hated the whole idea of my birth mum whilst at the same time feeling really sorry for her as the rape was not her fault.

I questioned who I was and why I had been born at all. As we lived in a Christian family and all attended church, I recall my adoptive mum telling me that how I was viewed by God was the most important thing to remember; that He loved me and believed I was precious and special. But I really struggled with this. I had so many questions and so much anger. Why had this happened to me? Why had God allowed it? I used to get angry with God and blame Him for it. In my mind it is, and always will be, the worst way for any life to begin.

Even in those early years I constantly fought with the idea that I could be anything or anyone special. As I had started life in such a repulsive manner it made me somehow feel like I was dirty. I was a mistake, the product of something far from good. How could anything good come from that? People used to constantly tell me that I was not an accident and that it must have been God's will for me to be born. But none of it made any difference to how I felt about me. I did not like me. I did not love me. I did not love where I had come from or what I knew about myself. In fact I hated it. There didn't seem to be much hope. I was angry that I was alive and I took that out on everyone. Especially myself.

I now know that it is very, very rare for a child conceived in those circumstances to be kept by the mother. But at the time I just felt the ugliness of the rejection and the pain of the knowledge I now had about my conception and my birth.

My behaviour continued to deteriorate and, as I got older this had a more negative impact on our family life.

Secondary school

When I first started secondary school I was in the old Lymm Grammar School building. The school was split over two sites and the plan was to move to a larger building down the road. We were moved a year after I started secondary school. I had just begun to find my way around and then everything changed. I found this really disruptive and didn't cope well. I operated best when I was in a set routine, and handled change poorly. I don't think this helped me with my behaviour.

I continued to really struggle at secondary school and found myself spending large amounts of time outside of classes. I had a reputation for being disruptive. Because I was outside the room I used to miss what was being taught, then the next time I was in that lesson I didn't follow what the teacher was doing because it was so often linked to the previous lesson. So I messed around again. It was a vicious circle. At the age of 12 I just resigned myself to the fact that I would be leaving the class imminently so put no effort in.

Isolated

Around this time at secondary school there was a room on the top floor where pupils who were struggling with either behaviour or learning were put. I began to spend most of my time there. Being isolated from the rest of my classmates and being put with other disruptive pupils didn't help me to develop friendships early on in secondary school. I think there was even an old school rumour that a ghost was at the top of the building too, which didn't help. There was also a massive stigma attached with going up there. People used to call me 'Thicko' and other derogatory terms.

In 'The Room' I was set really easy work. I still struggled massively with maths and never managed to get beyond the most basic level. I was better at English and found this slightly more interesting so worked a bit harder at that. My behaviour was mainly attention seeking; calling out when the teacher was talking, throwing things, eating, or basically anything that would annoy the teacher.

My sister Jo

One person that God used consistently to reach me and show me love was my sister, Jo. She was always amazing with me even during my most extreme behaviour. She would spend hours chatting to me, come to find me when I stormed off and chat to me when I had burned my bridges with other family members. There was something about her that meant I trusted her in a different way. Others in the family did try to help and made a real effort with me but for some reason it was Jo that I turned to and listened to. She was able to reason with me, get me to see things from other perspectives and often managed to win me round, just by being fair. She was amazing with the foster children too. It is perhaps no surprise that she went on to train to be a nursery nurse at what was then one of

Manchester's best nursery nurse training schools. She also went on to adopt four children of her own. I see now what an incredible mother she is and how she and her husband Phil are amazing parents to my wonderful nieces and nephews who, like me, for various reasons could not be kept by their birth parents.

You have to be a special person to be able to foster and adopt children. My mum, dad, sister and her husband have that incredible quality.

My behaviour was so extreme and volatile that no one could really plan or strategise a way to deal with me. As I grew up and got a bit wiser, I realised this and started to play games to mess with people's plans and ideas to 'manage' me. I was not hugely academic but I was starting to display a sort of cunning, sneaky behaviour that I would use to frustrate any efforts to 'sort me out'. I was unwilling to bend to anyone else's rules.

Stand up and be counted

My parents were heavily involved in the life of Lymm Baptist Church. Alongside some other families from there, we went to a large Christian conference called Spring Harvest several times when I was younger. It was run at a Butlin's site and was always a bit of an adventure. I used to be packed off to the children's venue. The leaders would try to get us all playing games, learning Bible stories and singing songs. I know they were doing their best, but it wasn't my thing at all. In truth I used to really struggle with it. The venue was huge and had lots of people from all over the country there. I hated having to mix with people I didn't know and would often leave the session early and wander off alone. After the main Spring Harvest event there used to be a reunion gathering organised in Manchester at the Free Trade Hall in the centre of the city. It was similar in style to the Big Top meeting with some worship and some teaching from the Bible. One year Mum and Dad decided we should go. The whole family went. It was pretty boring but, of course, I could not be trusted to stay at home alone.

A guy called Pete Meadows got up on the stage. He said he wanted to share something he felt God was saying to him. Then he asked my brother and me to stand up. I was very uncertain he had the right people; we both were. But we stood up, slowly, anyway. Then he spoke over us the following words:

"Even though things are hard for you right now, God is going to use you to reach thousands of young people."

He then prayed for us and got everyone to break into groups to pray for us too.

What a statement to make over someone like me! My mum remembered thinking he must have meant just my brother as at the time my behaviour made it hard to see how those words could have had anything to do with me.

I think it made my parents proud. After the event we were taken to the Dutch Pancake House which was my favourite restaurant at the time. I always chose a massive pancake on a huge plate with waffles, ice cream and chocolate sauce for puddings. We only went there on special occasions. Looking back, this was definitely a special occasion. After receiving the prophecy I felt proud for a bit. It was nice to have been singled out in front of lots of other Christians. I had no idea then how significant it would be.

Fred

As I look back over those first few years of my childhood, I can see now that God placed some very strategic people around me who loved me and supported me. Over the road from our house lived an elderly man called Fred and his wife Olwen. He was from the North East and had a heavy Geordie accent that I used to find difficult to understand sometimes.

Fred was part of our church and I used to go and help with his garden because he had bad knees. He was a great guy to know. He used to work at Sellafield Nuclear Plant and would spend ages telling me tall stories about what he used to do there. I am sure some of them were vastly exaggerated to capture my attention!

Mum and Dad always seemed happy for me to go over to see Fred. I think it gave them a break and they knew I was happy and safe over there. He also had a Jaguar car, which, for a young boy like me, was totally amazing. I loved it when he took me out in it. Olwen was quite ill and I think it must have been hard for Fred to look after her and perhaps I took his mind off it for a while, but he never complained. In fact, despite the physical hardships they suffered as they got older, Fred and Olwen never stopped talking about God. They would make me a drink and something to eat and then they would sit and read bits of the Bible to me. I guess this was one of the early times I remember Christians being different. As the years went by lots of people like Fred and Olwen got alongside me. I would say the ones that seemed to get through to me were the Christians. I guess their faith gave them a hope. I sensed it, and was always drawn to it.

Grandma

Another person who spent ages praying for me was my mum's mum. We used to go and stay with my Grandma and Grandpa in the holidays from time to time. And they visited us a bit too. When we visited, either just with my sisters and brother, or as a family, I was generally a nightmare getting into arguments with members of my family over silly things. Again there was something very different about my Grandma's attitude to me.

Where others would express their annoyance at me and my behaviour, she had a real patience. She would sit and talk to me and ask me why I behaved so badly. She would pray with me and was always quoting the Bible to me.

Looking back at all these people, and particularly the Christians who had patience with me, it is easy to see God's hand at work. Even in those very early years when I was perhaps the farthest from God, He was putting people in my path to influence me and show me that despite all that was happening He had a plan for my life.

CHAPTER 2

Nuisance

"Here's to the crazy ones. The misfits. The rebels. The trouble-makers. The round heads in the square holes. The ones who see things differently. They're not fond of rules. And they have no respect for the status-quo. You can quote them. Disagree with them. Glorify, or vilify them. But the only thing you can't do is ignore them. Because they change things. They push the human race forward. And while some may see them as the crazy ones, we see genius. Because the people who are crazy enough to think they can change the world are the ones who do".

Steve Jobbs

Frustrations

As I progressed through high school my behaviour and my attitude worsened. I became more and more isolated and I had few 'friends' in the true sense of that word. The people I hung out with were mostly drop-outs and misfits like me. My reputation as a troublemaker grew.

I put no effort into my schoolwork and never really completed any tasks that teachers set for me. At Lymm High School, pupils were encouraged to aim high with the motto 'Working together to achieve success'. I wanted none of that! I didn't want to work *with* anyone and I wasn't sure I was capable of any kind of *success*. In comparison, my brother and sisters worked hard, behaved well and achieved good grades. Teachers openly said to me, with no small degree of hostility, "Why can't you be more like them?" The staff who had day-to-day contact with me were increasingly frustrated by my lack of interest and deliberately difficult behaviour.

I used to find any reason I could to avoid doing the work that had been set. I frequently 'lost' my homework between school and home, usually in a bush on the walk home.

Fights

At this point I started to really wind up the older pupils. I was on a self-destruct mission and this seemed to be the next, rather illogical, step. The older kids were obviously far less tolerant than the younger guys. They did not appreciate the 'new kid' asserting himself. I spent large parts of my day when not in lessons, hiding from older lads I had been taunting. Occasionally, my brother Toby would offer me some much-needed protection. He was one of the hardest lads in his year and wasn't afraid of a fight, unlike me. Strangely, I was not actually all that good at fighting; I was all mouth.

My first fight was a short-lived one. I had been provoking a boy for weeks saying I was going to 'batter' him. One day on the way home from school, surrounded by loads of his mates, he ambushed me. Without warning, he came flying at me like a madman and punched me in the mouth. I remember going crazy and trying to clout him back, but there were so many people jostling and shoving that I couldn't get to him.

At my high school, like many today, there was a strange pack mentality. When a fight happened, people used to leg it from all over the school and crowd round shouting encouragement to the fighters until a teacher came or someone had given in. I never really liked these skirmishes but I had a few 'necessary' scraps with people in school. I soon learnt that this was not going to be 'my thing.' I was cleverer than that.

Family

Much to my parents' dismay, I spent large amounts of time sitting outside the Deputy Head's office. He had a table there where I used to sit, staring at the wall. The work he gave me was usually dull and tedious, like copying something down or filling in simple worksheets. It wasn't that I couldn't do the work - I just could not be bothered. At this time, I was creating lots of issues at home and I think some of this impacted on school. If I had an ongoing argument at home (which happened frequently) I would go to school angry and take it out on the teachers. The Deputy Head, Mr Mortishire, was also a member of the church we went to so I saw him most Sundays too!

Faking it

Lymm High School was very sport oriented. Surprisingly, I actually enjoyed some aspects of this side of school life. Being strong and wiry, I soon realised I was a gifted short distance runner. I was even encouraged to represent Lymm at inter-school events in the 100 and 200 metres. I was also good at long jump, hurdles and high jump. I really put a lot of effort into this and enjoyed the praise I received. Acclaim of any kind was so rare in those days and I secretly thrived on it.

However, not all sports appealed to me. I hated cross country running with a passion. The teachers found it hard that I would not even try. Because I was a strong sprinter, they assumed I would be a competent jogger. In reality, I was a hopeless distance runner and was out of breath after 200 metres. Part of the route took us through some woods near school. After a while I discovered that I could hide in the trees while everyone ran past. Because the route was circular I would wait till everyone had run past me, hang about in the wood for a while then head back the way we had come and hide by the school gates. As everyone was arriving I would join the breathless stragglers at the end, adding a bit of deep breathing and groans of my own to look tired when in fact I had probably only run 800 metres. I was quite proud of this little scam!

Foul play

Another sport we played was rugby. I hated both rugby and football. It always seemed to rain when we played and the pitches were freezing. I was put on the wing because I was a fast runner. Unfortunately, both sports gave the opportunity for me to be made me a target. What I hadn't bargained for was that both football and rugby gave my enemies the ideal opportunity to tackle me HARD. I was fouled many times as revenge for my cheek earlier in the day.

Fags

I started smoking at the age of 11 and quickly became addicted. Oddly, the first thing I tried was a pipe. An older lad who I used to give cheek to had started smoking one. (Looking back, this was a very weird thing for him to have done)! I encountered him once on Longbutt Lane (yes, it was called that. And yes, we found the name funny!).

Randomly, on this particular day, he offered me some tobacco. I inhaled and smoked loads of the strange, heady-smelling stuff. A little while later I went home and was violently sick. I can still remember the weird smell and the fact that the bathroom stank of old man pipe smoke. I'm sure Mum and Dad suspected what I had done, although it was never talked about. Vomiting that hard put me off pipes for life.

Sadly though, I progressed on to cigarettes and in order to get money for them I would do anything. Stealing from mum's purse was not uncommon but it was never enough. Then, one day, an entrepreneurial idea came to me. This is not something that I am proud of, but I worked out that if I shoplifted on the way to school I could sell whatever I had 'lifted' surreptitiously. So I used to sneak into the shop on the way into school with my bag, grabbing what I could and then selling it to people in form time. Soon I was making a nice little chunk of cash. People used to place orders and I took great pleasure in fulfilling them. This enterprising streak continued to develop.

In disguise

One day a couple of friends and I decided we wanted some beer. The trouble with Lymm was that everyone knew everyone else, and that included shopkeepers, so we hatched a plan. We would dress up as old men and go into the Gateway supermarket in the village and buy some beer. So we borrowed coats from our dads and put on some of their suit trousers. Finally we put talcum powder in our hair to make us look aged. Then we shuffled into the shop, hunched up. Walking over to the beer section as confidently as we could, we picked up a few cans each and went over to the counter to pay. I am convinced the staff must have suspected something and we were all really anxious as we waited to pay. But we got away with it. We shuffled out of the shop and then that evening went off somewhere and drank our prized beers. Quite a lot of my behaviour was of this ilk. I was always pushing the boundaries and looking for the next hustle that would earn us a few pounds; usually to pay for cigarettes or alcohol.

Because I was a bit of a daredevil and was easily led, I was often the first to try whatever scam we had come up with. At this age I did steal a lot. Sometimes I felt guilty but I got very good at convincing myself not to worry and justified my actions.

Under the radar

Following on from my continued poor behaviour and poor attendance, I had discovered I could skip lessons and disappear off into the woods. I used to make sure I attended only the lessons I liked; so I never missed woodwork, music or sport (that did not involve a football or a rugby ball).

There were things I got quite good at within school and certain teachers really tried to develop me in these areas. One of my favourite things has always been playing drums. My music teacher was incredibly patient with me and because good behaviour equalled practice time in the music house, I made sure I was good for him. Soon I started playing in the school orchestra and in musical productions.

I really enjoyed this because it earned me praise and people always seemed impressed with my playing. I used to revel in this as it was rare for my peers to speak well of me. I remember one year we had a carol service at the church over the road from school. At the time my behaviour was not great and I was told if I did not improve, I would not be allowed to play. I decided to push this threat to the limit and was subsequently not allowed to play. Another rival drummer from school was drafted in and this really hurt my feelings.

At school I also enjoyed tennis and any athletics and I really applied myself in these areas. I generally complied with PE teachers as they seemed a bit stricter than the other teachers and I respected their fitness levels... perhaps to the point where I was actually nervous they could catch me!

Under the curse

I remember one day I was messing around in the changing room. The teacher was trying to explain what we would be doing that day and I wasn't listening. This teacher turned to me in front of the whole group (I remember it being a lot of pupils because we joined other classes for sport). He said, "Spurling you are a waste of time and you will never become anything!"

This really stung me and I remember pupils taking the mick out of me for weeks. I knew that teachers found me hard work and suspected that they used to say all sorts of things about me in the staff room, but this was the first time it had been done in front of other kids. It really went on to affect me. I carried the sting of those words for years.

That 'curse' spoken over me so cruelly and publically, humiliated me and made me begin to give up on even the small achievements in my life. I could no longer see the point of school. If I was never going to amount to anything, there was no point in trying. I gave up and decided to make myself as difficult as I could. Steadily my behaviour got even worse at school and at home. People seemed to be growing tired of me, even those who had made the effort with me before seemed to get frustrated. It was a self-fulfilling prophecy. It had been declared over me that I was a waste of everyone's time and I tried hard to prove it. I started skipping lessons more and more.

Under the bed

On one occasion Toby, one of his friends and I decided to wag some lessons. We decided to go home. Remember that Dad was a travelling sales rep; he was in and out all day depending on what his diary was like. Sometimes he would be out for the whole day working in a nearby city like Liverpool or Leeds. On this day I believe we thought he was out further afield. It was easy to hear when Dad left the house because he always very distinctively took ages to change from first to second gear and you could hear the revs rising. It was not as easy to hear him returning. This was a distinct disadvantage to two boys who frequently misbehaved and gave their mum constant hassle. Anyway, on this day we did not hear him return. I was in my room and Toby was in the lounge with his mate. I had stormed off because Toby and his mate Nick kept giving me dead arms and play fighting with me. They had heard a car and managed to scarper down the alley near our house. They had 'forgotten' to let me know this and the next thing I heard was Dad's key in the door. I spent the rest of the day hidden under my bed. Every time I tried to leave the bedroom the door creaked really loudly. I quickly abandoned getting out and lay under the bed hiding until Dad went out a few hours later. I'd like to say this taught me a lesson and I never wagged it again, but sadly it was now a game and I played by my own rules.

Under the Doctors

Around this time, because my behaviour was such a concern both in and out of school, I was referred to an Educational Psychologist. My visits took me to a building next to the Golden Gates in Warrington. I liked going because I was taken out of school to go there. They used to ask me lots of questions and make me draw pictures to try and illustrate how I felt about certain things. Being a creative soul, I liked to give them something to talk about. I knew what I was doing and played lots of games with them.

One day, I remember being asked to draw a house and put things in it that I liked. I drew the outline of the house, then slowly and deliberately picked up a black crayon and scribbled over the whole of the house. The person leading the session asked me why I had done that and I gave no answer. I quickly worked out that I could stump them by doing random things like this. 'Messing with them' became a regular feature of my sessions. I never did or said anything particularly malicious or drew anything hugely concerning but I did like the feeling of control I had when I was able to frustrate the session psychologist by not complying. I thought it was fun to act up like this. I had no idea that my silly games would have the impact that they did. This was my first experience of psychologists. It would not be my last.

As my behaviour got worse in school it also deteriorated at home. I was gradually isolating myself from everyone and whilst I would say that my family never gave up or kept trying to build bridges, there were now regular periods of time where my behaviour at home made life difficult for everyone. As I said earlier, my anger and aggression were particularly directed towards my mum. I would often explode with anger, usually over something trivial. I did not link these feelings at the time with my adoption or issues surrounding feeling abandoned. I just thought it was how I felt. I would be in a mood for a few days and regularly blanked my family and refused to interact. As I hated change I was also really bad at dealing with anything that was not routine. So family holidays or trips to see relatives were a time when I was particularly challenging.

The biggest change

One day I was told that a meeting had been called at school. Mum and Dad were to attend too. I remember waiting outside the Headteacher's office with my parents. There wasn't much to say. I tapped my feet and swung on my chair. I had been here before, many, many times. They were called in first and after a little while I was asked to go in too. I had been in frequent meetings with my parents and teachers; I did not think this was any different.

But the atmosphere in the room surprised me. This time I sensed something different was going on but had no idea what. I looked around me at the faces, but couldn't get any clues.

I was informed, out of the blue, that aged fourteen I was being excluded from Lymm High School. My attitude and disruptive behaviour was too hard for them to manage. Other parents were unhappy that I was affecting their children's learning. This was the end of the road.

I stared, hard-faced and tight-lipped at the Head as he spoke the words. They didn't sink in. I shot a sideways look at my parents. Neither of them looked up.

A huge rush of anxieties filled my brain, screaming for room. Where was I being sent? Was it far away? How would I handle it?

I sat in silence as my 'sentence' was read out. Sullen, quiet and looking as though I was not bothered - but inside I was terrified.

The school had looked into alternative education for me in Cheshire but the local 'Special School' was full. Having seen my Educational Psychologist's report Warrington Borough Council had decided that they were 'unable to educate me'. Suddenly those little games I had played in the sessions did not seem quite so funny.

The authorities had looked at local alternatives and none were available, so my parents and I were told that I would be leaving the area.

I had my systems for coping: my shop-lifting, my drums, my mates and I had my family.

For the first time, in a very long time, I felt truly afraid. It was the sort of fear that dumped itself on me like a great weight – all at once with no warning. I felt physically sick.

The biggest fear

The Head told me that I was being moved to a residential unit in Shropshire. This was the only place they could find for me. My poor parents were devastated. There was no alternative. They, of course, wanted me to be educated closer to home, but I had burnt all of my bridges. I was 'un-educate-able' if that is even a word. This was my only option.

There have been a few occasions in my life where I have thought, "What on *earth* have I done?" and this was one of them. It really was the end of the road.

I hated change.

I hated having no choice.

I hated authority figures.

I hated being told what to do and where to go.

So it's fair to say that this turn of events was not easy for me to handle. It was also very traumatic for my family, especially my mum. Looking back now, I know that this was the last thing she would have wished for me.

Leaving the familiarity of the village I had lived in for nearly twelve years was a terrifying thought. The prospect of sharing a house with other people who didn't know me, and didn't know my needs, was the worst thing I could imagine. Everything I knew and held on to as my only source of comfort was to be taken away.

Separation

A few days later Mum and Dad drove me to Hilltop Boarding and Therapeutic School in Ludlow, Shropshire. I was due to meet the Headmaster and be shown around. On the surface the Head was a real character. He seemed very bubbly and jovial, but something made me suspect that if you got on the wrong side of him a huge powerful shout would be unleashed. It was a truth I discovered on numerous subsequent occasions.

I was shown around the buildings. The living area looked a little like a large, old nursing home. There were lots of bedrooms, TV rooms, a dining room and two lounges. There was even a smoking room and a couple of psychologists' offices based at the top of the building. Lucky me!

I met the chef and she seemed really friendly, and the caretaker seemed friendly enough too. (I later went on to realise that with all the damage we did to the building he was probably the busiest member of staff.) Across the car park, hidden away behind some trees was the school. It was a series of temporary classrooms with a woodwork area and a music room. The staff in the school all seemed nice enough but I got the sense I wasn't going to be particularly challenged there. The school had some pupils in it when I was looking round. They all seemed to be behaving. I would soon realise that this was not always the case.

Inside I had a sinking feeling. This was going to be my home and my life for…in truth I had no idea how long I'd be there. I followed the Head around trying to look interested, and remember what he was saying, but I was already feeling that raw sense of panic I get every time something changes in my life. I did perk up slightly when I was shown the indoor swimming pool and the music room, though. At least there would be some things I could get into.

But this was no luxury hotel; the place was tired and old. Paintwork was peeling and lots of things were broken and more than a little 'lived in'. It looked beaten up. But it was not a cheap option - it cost my local authority £7,000 per month to send me there.

One thing I wish I had asked at this stage (although it would not have made any difference) was, "What are the other pupils who live here like?". Hilltop specialised in taking pupils from all over the country that local authorities could not handle. There were many examples of disturbing behaviour all around me. Some wild and very broken young people found themselves at Hilltop, as bewildered and as odd as me and much, much more so.

Most of the pupils at Hilltop exhibited very challenging behaviour as a result of their personal circumstances. Some were victims of domestic or sexual abuse, some were young offenders and others had behavioural challenges or learning difficulties and others, like me, exhibited attachment disorders.

Hurt, abused, damaged children and young people are challenging to be around. I found that out to my cost many, many times.

Shortly after the visit I was assigned a social worker and in my mind this meant I was now 'in care'. The thought was once again one of total rejection. Being 'in care' implied that no-one wanted me or could handle me. It felt like I was going backwards, back to what I had come from. My life had started in care and to end up there again was a kick in the teeth, even though I knew I had no-one but myself to blame. I often thought about my mum and dad and felt how lucky I was to have them. Their support and their love for me did not change even at the times when my behaviour was appalling. They still believed in me and wanted the best for me. I knew it was hard for them that I had ended up here and I suspected that they had only made the decision to let me go after a lot of discussion and prayer. They knew that my needs were not being met at Lymm and Mum said she frequently felt sad that, despite her constant battle to get me an education near home, it had come to this and it was now my only option. I had failed them. After all they had given me I had failed them and myself. And the system had failed me.

The social worker I had been given was not very helpful. My mum (who was also a social worker) agreed with me on this. It terrified me that the person meant to be looking after me and caring for me was not great at their job. It made me feel so insecure to think that I could already see so many flaws appearing in my 'care'. But it didn't make any difference. A few days later my stuff was packed and I was on my way. My behaviour was awful that day as I was so upset and did not know how to show it appropriately. I sat in the car and tried hard not to talk or to cry. I felt little, insignificant, angry and afraid. The worst change in my life was on its way. For the next two years Hilltop was to be my home.

Finding my feet

On arrival I was shown my room. I was annoyed to find I had to share with another lad called James. He was out at the time. I quickly discovered that James was a glue sniffer with a bad temper. When he arrived home he was not too happy about me being in his room. We didn't really hit it off. In fact, we hit each other. We had a fight a couple of days later.

I was assigned a key worker called Aaron, a black lad from Birmingham. He went on to be an amazing support to me but I did not make life easy for him. Poor bloke!

My first meal was interesting. I went down to the dining room, stood at the hatch, got some food and sat at a table. A few minutes later a cockney voice behind me shouted, "Oi! That's my seat! Shift!"

Not knowing any better I stated that I was not moving. The guy lost it, picked up a brush and smacked me over the back with it. I flew at him, knocking the table over as I tried to punch him. Darren, I later discovered, was not someone who liked to be told what to do. Most people let him get away with whatever he wanted. He had been involved in gang stuff in London and had a reputation for bullying.

Developing my reputation

It felt good that I had defended myself, but I quickly learned that I had to keep my wits about me and know who my enemies were. Vulnerable, volatile young people being in such close proximity meant that fights and arguments were an explosive daily event. I soon learnt that I needed to copy the other residents' behaviour to cope. I developed an even more violent temper that was regularly becoming out of control. I would flare up at the slightest thing that offended me. I was now 14 and I was growing physically stronger. It often took 3 or 4 staff to control me when I got aggressive.

Increasingly I found myself in the 'calm down' room. This was right on the other side of the house so if I kicked off in the kitchen, I was pretty much dragged there by force. Once in the room I would punch the walls, spit at the staff and generally hurt anyone who was around. On one occasion I got so mad that I hurt my back and ended up on my bed in agony for a few days.

Another time I lost it because I was told I was not allowed any pocket money because my name had been in the 'Sanctions Book' too many times for walking out of lessons. Angrily, I stormed into the main building, walked up to a window and smashed my forearm into it, breaking the glass. As I ran off I was chased by lots of staff. Hiding round the back of the school, I looked down and saw blood dripping down my hand onto the floor. I was shocked by what I had done. The hole in my arm was very deep and it was starting to hurt badly. The anger and adrenaline started to wear off. I felt faint. I was eventually taken to casualty and told the cut was too wide to stitch. They dressed it but it took a long time to heal. I still have a dent under my skin where it happened.

As my time at Hilltop went on my behaviour worsened but I was actually fairly popular with staff as I was not the most extreme case there. I didn't apply myself to the schoolwork set and frequently just walked out and went off into town. But I was not as troublesome as some. A large percentage of the other residents had really horrible backgrounds. We had a couple of teenage prostitutes, a teenage sex offender and various other unsociable characters. At the back of my mind, despite the fact that I was a very angry young man, I understood that I had had a the bebefit of a much better upbringing than most.

There was a lot of sex going on. It was a mixed house and many of the residents had the kind of background where casual sexual activity was normal. But God must have been watching over me. I never got involved in any of this sexual behaviour. I felt strongly that I would wait. I think I also had issues with the idea of having sex because of how I had been conceived.

Holiday times

Most holidays we were taken away somewhere by the staff. It was usually just more of the same bad behaviour in a caravan instead of the house. They used something called 'Crisis Intervention' if you got really bad. The offender would be taken away with a couple of staff members to camp somewhere really remote. They would make you do something physically demanding. You were really pushed there so I avoided going. I was clever and knew how to wind the staff up but would back off just before it got me into too much trouble.

'Borrowing' a car

At the school they had a Volvo 340 GLT that was used to ferry us around and take us to appointments. There was a forest in Ludlow and some of the staff would let us drive in the car park or down forest tracks. I had always been fascinated by cars and loved the feeling that driving gave me. I even did a work experience placement at a local Rover garage; I went for a week and really enjoyed it. It was a good laugh even though the male mechanics swore like troopers. All week they kept saying that before I left they were going to 'grease my nuts'. I remember thinking this seemed a little bit over familiar and being slightly fearful all week. Fortunately nothing happened.

I was also sent to a local college where we were taught bricklaying and plastering. I quickly realised I was not destined to be Britain's next master house builder. I was useless at it.

Over time I got quite confident at handling cars and especially the school Volvo, and reckoned I could drive it myself.

One day another pupil and I decided we would take the Volvo for a little spin down a real road. We 'borrowed' the keys from the safe and set off down the lanes near school. We drove it around for quite a while then left it in a small road behind the school. Back in the office we triumphantly put the keys back without being seen. Or so we thought.

A short time later we were called into the Head's office.

"Spurling! Where is the Volvo?" he almost spat out the words.

I looked at the floor, unwilling to appear in the slightest compliant in front of my friend.

"Don't know." I mumbled. "Why you askin' me?"

He shouted again, "Where is the car? Where is it now, Spurling? You were seen driving it! You can't deny it. If you don't tell me immediately I will call the police!"

After the most savage shouting Mr Wainwright had ever dished out, we reluctantly showed him where the car was.

We were well punished for our misdemeanour. We didn't get any pocket money for a few weeks nor were we allowed on any trips or activities for a while. We were told that if we pulled a stunt like that again we would be moved to another school.

I knew this was unlikely because there wasn't a huge amount of other places to send me. Also the man was being paid to look after me. Why else would he do his job?

Driving without a license on a main road in a stolen car without insurance was probably not my best moment. But even at the time I knew I had done it to impress others. I chose not to repeat that particular offence.

Up in flames

On another occasion I was smoking in my bedroom (this was not allowed but we all did it). Next to my bed I had an old-fashioned lamp with tassels on it. For reasons I still can't explain I deliberately flicked the lighter under one of the tassels. In a second the whole lamp was alight! I managed to unplug it but didn't have anything to put out the fire.

The next thing I heard was the loud fire alarms going off. People were moving out of the building. The alarms were linked to the local fire station. We knew this because other pupils and I frequently set them off and the engines would come. Some of the kids used to enjoy wasting their time. The fire fighters came and put out the small fire. They lifted the floorboards and removed some of the skirting to check that the fire had not spread. The fire had destroyed the light and badly burnt a section of the carpet. As you can imagine, I was far from popular that night.

It wasn't long before I was in the Headteacher's office yet again being asked to explain why I had done it. The truth was I just hadn't thought it through. I got another massive telling off and was sanctioned for a while with no money and no activities allowed.

More psychology

As part of my time at Hilltop we had to go and chat to two psychologists. They came in every few days and if you had been particularly badly behaved you were sent for extra sessions with them. I played the same strategy I did with the Educational Psychologists I had been referred to in Warrington, giving them the answer they wanted to hear, or mucking about in their sessions. If they touched a raw nerve about my past I would explode and walk out. I quickly decided that I didn't really want to deal with my issues and having people trying to get me to talk about the reason I was adopted would be done on my terms when I was ready.

Looking back now I can see that there were some amazing staff at the school. Dora, the bursar, was like a mother to us and used to really make sure we were well fed and had clothes. Rowena was another kind lady. She worked in the office and knew everything about the place. She liaised with all the social workers and was the person you went to if you wanted to speak to them. She was also very caring and you could tell it was more than a job to her and she used to sometimes take me out off site. I would go and join in with what she was doing with her two daughters. It was nice sometimes just to get out of school and do things normal families would do. Her daughter, Talitha, was really funny - and good-looking too - which was a bonus.

A few teachers stood out as well. My class teacher, Peter, was one of the most patient people I had ever met. He regularly took pupils home to his house for tea. He was also into music and played guitar. Regularly we would go into the music room where I would drum and he would play electric guitar. He really encouraged me musically and it was his influence that led to me being allowed to take a drum kit into a space in the gym so I could practice in peace. I took a real pride in this kit and eventually, much to the dislike of other pupils, I was allowed to have it in my bedroom. I used my drumming as a way of channelling my aggression and found it to be a really good way to get my frustrations out. Whilst it never took very long for them to resurface it kept me happy and busy some of the time. The school also organised for me to have golf lessons at the local club. I was pretty good at golf as I had played this before when I lived in Lymm. I used to love smashing the ball as far as I could. Again it was a form of escapism and a way of getting rid of pent up energy.

I stayed at Hilltop for two years from the age of 14-16. Unsurprisingly, I left with absolutely no qualifications. I never applied myself educationally. Around this time my parents came to see me and we had a meeting with the Headteacher and my social worker. At this stage I still did not know what would happen to me. Anyone else who left and didn't return to their parents or carer ended up in a 'halfway house'. These were houses in towns near Birmingham. You lived there, semi-independently, with staff on hand to help you adjust to life out on your own.

At the meeting something was said that Mum took exception to. Mum was very determined when she made her mind up. She told them in no uncertain terms that I would be going home to live with them again. So that is what happened. A few days later I said a very emotional goodbye to the staff who had been my family for the last two years of my life. Saying farewell to the other pupils was hard too. Although we constantly fought each other and many people had come and gone, it was sad to say goodbye to some of them. It was the end of a chapter. The hardest people to leave behind were Dora, Rowena and my class teacher. All of them had really believed in me. I did go back to visit a couple of times in the months afterwards, but things had moved on by then.

Strangely, I was recently in Shropshire and took a drive past my old school. I found it ironic to read on the sign that it has now become a luxury country hotel!

God was looking after me in those two years at Hilltop. He protected me from getting into any deep relationships that would cause me, or others, long-term harm. He helped me develop my drumming and my fitness and He even reminded me that I was loved and precious to my family. Whilst

I had no GCSEs to my name, I knew that I was not a total failure. I even felt a little bit expectant about what was to come. My family wanted me back and that was an amazing feeling. My mum had fought for me. She and Dad loved me.

I was going home.

CHAPTER 3

Training ground

After Hilltop, I returned home. By now, my family had moved from Lymm, in Cheshire, to Rusholme, in Manchester.

I recently met with my eldest sister. We chatted about her early memories of me and how my adoption into the family felt for her as we all grew up. When I started high school my eldest sister Nikki was in sixth form. She was heavily involved in the school Christian Union and was regularly part of a team giving assemblies. Like any other 17-year-old she was often out at parties and socialising with her friends. I remember her having on/off boyfriends. When we spoke recently Nikki said she vaguely remembered picking me up from the children's home when she was six years old. She has memories of family holidays and us always being in her life after our adoption. She said she saw us to be as much her siblings as she did her sister Jo because we had always been there from an early age.

At times Nikki really struggled with my poor behaviour and felt protective towards her mum and dad. Sometimes she felt angry about the way I behaved, but always loved me regardless as I was her little brother. She never really felt any regrets about having adopted brothers. One day Nikki recalled someone making a racist comment during her form time at school and she had memories of reacting strongly. Her response left the pupil in question in no doubt that she would not tolerate that language in front of her. Mum and Dad constantly reiterated to us all that skin colour did not define you. We were all viewed the same, irrespective of colour.

A little while later when I ended up at Hilltop Nikki was down in Oxford training to be a nurse. She heard snippets of what went on with me but in the absence of mobile phones she only had limited contact via a payphone and visits back to Lymm, so she missed out on perhaps the wildest part of my teen years but she was still a sister I looked up to. I always felt proud of her training to be a nurse and like mum and my other sister Jo it isn't surprising to me that they all chose people-focused careers.

The decision to move to Rusholme was partly due to Dad's work, but was also a deliberate move on my parents' part to help us have a more multi-cultural environment. Living in Rusholme, this was certainly the case. We were surrounded by people of every colour and culture. We no longer stuck out. Mum and Dad had bought a really nice house and I was given the converted loft space. I loved this room as it was spacious and very much my own. I had my own kettle up there, so it felt more like a flat at times.

One down side of the house we lived in was that Rusholme was a stone's throw away from Maine Road, Manchester City's old home ground. On match days the roads near our house were packed with cars. Local thieves would regularly come and smash windows and steal the car stereos. Dad had his car broken into a few times and had the stereo stolen. But on the whole the house worked for us as a family and I felt quite settled there - for a while anyway.

One thing Mum and Dad were very clear about was the need for me to be proactive in looking for something to do with my life. I started applying for jobs but, as I had no qualifications, I was regularly knocked back. I also looked into doing YTS training, which was a bit like a modern day apprenticeship, but I didn't really have the motivation.

Filing error

Eventually I did start getting little bits of work. I went through a period of trying lots of different things to see what I was good at. I got jobs in offices, mainly as a 'dogsbody' junior. One such position was working at a solicitors firm as a filing clerk. I hated the boredom and being told what to do. To be honest it was a recipe for disaster. Put a lad with a logic disorder in an office full of 10,000 important files and stand well back! Understandably, I was in constant trouble for losing paperwork that the solicitors needed urgently for court. I didn't mean to misplace things, I just wasn't brilliant at remembering where they were!

Toddler on a mission

Early Christmas memories

Hot air balloon ride   *Primary school*

Jo, Toby, Me and Nikki

Me and Toby on holiday

Primary school creativity

NHS specs love

Home visit during my time at Hilltop

Primary School orchestra

Me, Jo and Toby on a family walk

Collecting an award at Hilltop

Me and Jo practice wedding shoot

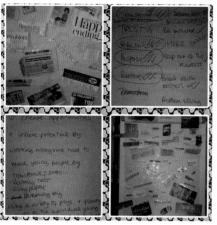

Thoughts from an N-Gage away day

Collecting the Chief Constable's Award from Sir Peter Fahy in 2008

Early N-Gage years Elevate Project

Shift Project at Didsbury Park

Early office days with Dad and Rachel Gaunt

Drumming

Petrol head

Amy and Me

Speaking at Ivy Fallowfield

Ella's dedication

My first parachute jump

Safely back on solid ground

Kayaking with Ella

My girls

Mum and Dad (Nan and Pops) with Ella

Catalyst in Baguley

Photoshop fun

A petrol head's dream come true -
the gift of a car

I take my food very seriously

Fog Lane fun day with the N-Gage truck

Panda head

Catering

After a few attempts at various jobs I decided to try something completely different. It was then that I thought about training to be a chef. I'd always liked cooking and decided to enrol in a college to study this.

I struggled for the first term because I wasn't used to academic learning. Having just left Hilltop where expectations of me were minimal, I quickly learnt that college would not tolerate my silly behaviour.

Because it was something I was vaguely interested in, I started applying myself and trying to do well. I figured this was better than failing at this as well. I battled with the written work but tried my best. I managed to stick this course out for two years. That was a real achievement and for the first time in my life, I hadn't walked away from something.

One of the tutors was a black guy called Carl. He was a West Indian with a really thick accent. We all found it hard to understand what he was saying most of the time, but it was clear he was really passionate about teaching catering. He believed in me and was someone who inspired me to try harder. He used to tell us stories of his days working in various kitchens all over the country. Something about him made me apply myself far more than I was used to doing. I found myself succeeding and doing well. It was a new feeling for me. I liked it.

As part of the course, we were sent on various placements. My first three were real eye openers. I quickly learnt that kitchens were lively places and that most head chefs had serious 'issues'! It wasn't long before I understood how to work, and even thrive, in that kind of environment.

My first placement was at the college. They had a restaurant for students to work in as they trained and we served both the students and the staff. I found my time there mundane because we made the same food every day and the menu wasn't particularly demanding or interesting. After a few weeks I was told I would be moving to a 'proper' restaurant. I was placed at one called 'Pier 6' in Salford Quays. Whilst it was hard to get to, I loved it there. The chef made me do lots of the boring jobs but it felt good to be in a proper fast-paced working kitchen for the first time.

As it was a steak restaurant I learnt a lot about how to cook meat to perfection. I really enjoyed this placement but was soon moved on to my next one.

This time, I was sent to the Manchester University Business School kitchens. This was a lot bigger and the expectations on me were a lot higher. The staff were all jokers and the head chef was a nutter who used to enjoy going for a few pints after work.

It was here that I learnt about how easy and fun it is to play tricks on the youngest or newest member of staff. One day they gave me a box of chillies and asked me to chop them up. There were loads of them and I had to do them fast. Unbeknown to me, they usually gave the person doing this task a pair of gloves. I was denied this 'little luxury'. After chopping the chillies to the best of my ability I decided I needed to go to the loo. Ouch! I have never experienced such a burning sensation as I did on that day. As I came out, everyone in the kitchen was in hysterics asking me "How's your man bits?" I swore at them, then joined in laughing, knowing that this was the best way to fit in.

I stuck at this career for a couple of years and by and large I really enjoyed it. The only downside was it really impacted on my new-found social life.

My behaviour at home was still an issue. I still had a terrible temper and my attitude towards other family members was pretty bad. For some reason I became very withdrawn at home and spent lots of time alone in my room. I was particularly harsh towards Mum and she and Dad struggled with both my poor attitude and my seemingly thoughtless behaviour.

Looking back, though, it was not thoughtless. In fact, I thought about a lot of things, but I found myself having very negative feelings about my adoption. The underlying issues I had around being 'given away' had not been fully dealt with at Hilltop or anywhere else. My anger, hurt and confusion were simply simmering away under the surface.

Finding Church

After about a year of being back at home, Mum and Dad decided that I needed to be plugged into a church-based youth group of some description. One day Mum took out the Yellow Pages and looked up some churches.

She found one called Ivy Cottage in Didsbury, South Manchester. Her sole reason for choosing this one was that the youth worker listed had the most unusual surname. Paul Vaswani, who was randomly picked from a phone book by my mum, had not been randomly picked by God. He was soon treated to my presence. Mum hauled me to a youth group meeting the very next Friday evening.

As I have already said, I hated going to new places and meeting new people. I remember being totally petrified. As I walked into the basement of the church, I found twenty teenagers all talking at once. As the door opened and I went in, everyone stopped talking and stared at me. The silence was horrible. Paul introduced me to everyone, "This is Christie. He may be joining our group."

I sat and didn't really say much that first evening. When I got home Mum asked me how I had got on. I mumbled that it was "OK" and went upstairs. On reflection, I think this so-called 'chance meeting' of a load of new people was a true God moment for me. I had no idea that Paul would, in time, become a real support and a close friend. But, of course, God knew. He understood what I needed and had picked exactly the right place and people for me.

The guys from the youth club seemed to accept me. They knew nothing of my story and I didn't feel the need to share anything at this stage. After a few weeks of going I gradually started getting to know people and found them all incredibly easy-going and friendly. If any of them were having a party I was always invited.

I started hanging around with a lad called Warren and his best friend Dave. They both lived in massive houses in Didsbury. I also noticed that the parents of all these new friends I was making were incredibly kind to me. Warren's mum took me under her wing a bit. Another new revelation was that some of the girls seemed to have taken a shine to me. This was a new thing and it was very pleasant. Could things be on the up for Christie Spurling? It certainly seemed that way.

As I threw myself into the youth group I also found myself accidentally starting to attend church too. We all went as a big crowd so it was easy to go along. We used to sit in the back corner and were probably a bit disruptive. But everyone was kind to me. I had been going to church all my life except for when I went to Hilltop. Was there something in this faith stuff? I became a little less dismissive of God and Christianity and even started to listen occasionally too.

I went out with a Christian girl called Emma for a while and this was my first proper relationship. We used to spend time talking about what had happened to me and it used to bug me that she always said stuff like, "God can heal you." Or, "If you talk to God about this stuff it will get better."

In fact pretty much everyone who found out my story at church seemed to be pointing me in that same direction.

Inside I was scared of fully committing my life to God. I guess I was worried that it wouldn't work out - like so many of the other things I had tried. But I just threw myself into serving at church. I joined the worship team and started playing the drums most Sundays. I loved doing this. It always amused me that I was really shy and introverted but would get up in front of 300 people and play the loudest instrument!

I also started helping with the children's work, mainly because Emma was involved, but I also liked to keep busy. Paul Vaswani became a real friend to me at this point. He used to take me out to play pool and we would chat through my issues and he would offer support. I was struck by how much time they all invested in me. Maria Fox and Wendy Robinson, who helped lead the youth work at Ivy, also invested a lot of time and effort in me too. It seemed people were really 'for me' and wanted to help and support me.

The day I said 'YES'

One Sunday evening at what felt like a fairly normal service, the guy preaching asked if anyone wanted to become a Christian. Inwardly I started to panic. What if I did this and it didn't work? Could I really trust God? Would He let me down? I remember feeling a bit lost but also strangely drawn to the idea that Jesus had died for my sins. Head bowed, the preacher said, "If you want to become a Christian, put your hand up and repeat this prayer."

My hand shot into the air. I prayed the prayer and someone came over and chatted to me and we prayed a bit more.

That was it!

I was a Christian now, so life would change, right?

Things did change but certainly not overnight. God needed to do a lot of work on me and I wasn't always willing to be worked on! I still had many issues around my adoption that needed to be dealt with. I also still felt pain because of what had happened to my real mum and was angry with the world for what had happened. It would be years before I eventually started to turn a corner on that score, but God now had me in His hand and He had a plan worked out for me that none of us could predict. What's more, I knew that and I believed it for the first time.

Moving out

I went home and told my parents what had happened and they were both thrilled. I knew that they (and lots of others) had been praying for me to make this kind of commitment for years and they were over the moon that it had finally happened. Unfortunately, now aged 17 and being a moody teenager, I was still hard work. Despite my new-found faith I was very difficult to manage and I didn't find it easy to be at home.

It was decided that I should move out and find myself somewhere to rent. I think since living at Hilltop I had found adjusting to family life again much too hard. At Hilltop I had learnt to look after myself. I was now older and wiser, and moving out, although difficult, was going to be best all round. Again it is important to say that this was a mutual decision and Mum and Dad fully supported me.

Through asking at church I managed to find a room to rent in Didsbury. The house was owned by an older guy who went to a local church. I had a room and shared the kitchen and bathroom. By now I was in one of the many periods of being unemployed. I just kept walking out of jobs at the first sign of being bored or of finding something hard.

I still loved catering but it paid rubbish money and entailed working long unsociable hours so I gave up on that. I had various office jobs but found them boring and rarely stuck at any of them. As I was also quite moody at this age I wasn't the greatest asset to a company. I carried on like this for quite a while. I stayed at the house, noticing that my money always ran out. The benefits I received were not enough to keep me going and I wanted to be out socialising with my friends and going to the pub.

I am ashamed to say that I started to steal to feed myself. I would shoplift smaller things like a pot noodle or anything that I could get in my pocket. Despite being a new Christian and feeling guilty about this, sometimes it felt like my only option.

It was quite lonely living in the house because the guy I shared with kept himself to himself. He was much older than me so we had little in common. People did come and visit me from time-to-time but I was far from happy. I stayed in that house for about a year.

Then I discovered that some lads from church all lived in a shared house in Withington. They had a room going spare and I worked out that with my benefits I could probably afford to move in. They were all older than me but only by a few years. Still not very confident, I shyly went for a look around. The house was huge and certainly well lived in. But I instantly felt that it was better than where I currently lived so a short time later I moved in. I was suddenly a whole lot happier. We all used to sit together in the kitchen at night and have a few drinks. There was a real mix of characters and because most of them worked I was able to get their advice. I hit it off really well with one guy called Dave. He was a real Manchester lad and told it like it was. He was also good at giving me advice and telling me to snap out of it when I was being a pain.

Around this time someone gave me a drum kit so I stuck it in the cellar and used to spend ages downstairs practicing. One of the other lads I shared with was a lad called Guy. He was probably the best blues guitarist I had ever heard and we used to spend a lot of time together jamming. The house next door was owned by the same people who owned ours. It was great because this house was full of girls. Over the time I was there both houses were full of young Christians.

It did me so much good to be in that environment and I really grew in my faith. I stayed there for a couple of years. I had various jobs and also periods of unemployment. I felt as though I was starting to change. I still felt angry and confused about my past but I was making headway.

I really struggled with the idea that God was a loving Father. I think this was linked to my perceived hatred for my real dad. Surely all dads were the same? I used to spend hours arguing and debating about the idea of suffering. Why did God let it happen? I also stated on numerous occasions that if God had planned to use me and my story to help others in the future, He should have asked me first!

I developed a vague interest in theology. I think this was more because I was very argumentative and it seemed an ok way to argue with other Christians. My Dad used to say to me, "Christie, when you grow up you should be a barrister because you are so good at arguing."

Mum and Dad moved away to Cambridge; my brother Toby was still nearby in Warrington; Jo, my youngest sister was in Peterborough; and my eldest sister Nikki was settled in Kent. Due to the distances we didn't really see each other that much. I never had much money so travelling to see people didn't really happen.

As I threw myself into church life and the youth group developed further, I found I had a bit more of a social life. At last I felt like I had some really good friends. We used to spend a fair bit of time going into town. I quickly discovered that I hated nightclubs. All the darkness and dinginess really didn't appeal to me. I also hated the air of suspicion you were treated with by the doormen who always looked 'Hench' and seemed to save their dirtiest looks for me.

I did however develop a real taste for alcohol. I discovered that this was a good way to forget things. So I started drinking a lot. If I am honest I think I have an addictive personality. I guess that when I was knocking back all that beer I wasn't really in a place where I wanted to care for myself.

When I was younger I had really not taken any pride in my appearance because I felt rejected. The neglect showed itself mainly in my teeth. At one point they were so bad that my front teeth had holes in them. I never smiled because I was so ashamed of my teeth. As I was starting to attract attention from girls I decided I needed to get them sorted. I made countless trips to the dental hospital in Manchester. Some of the work they had to do was excruciatingly painful, including three tooth extractions and lots of root canal work. On one visit I had to have 4 injections (this is where my phobia of needles must have started). But I decided to persevere and eventually I had a fairly normal set of teeth. This boosted my confidence no end. I felt more comfortable, was far less self-conscious at things like interviews and I managed to teach myself to smile.

I became even more heavily involved in the youth and children's work at church. I found it really rewarding and I seemed to be good at it and was really encouraged by lots of people to continue to do it. I just used to get involved and help run the games. I liked doing children's work slightly less because I felt you had to be willing to make a fool of yourself a bit more and I was self-conscious. At that time a lady called Anne helped run all the children's work. I was put into a home group with her, her husband Peter and a few other Christians. There was a mix of other people in the group and we used to meet to pray and chat about the sermon on Sunday. These people were to have a profound impact on me that would last many years, and is still so today. They took me under their wing and used to invite me for food before the meetings.

One day Anne, who worked as a Deputy Head, mentioned that they were looking for someone to go into her school to teach drums. Would I like to do it? Surprised and pleased, I found myself saying, "Erm…yes please. That would be amazing."

So I started going into her school one morning a week and was paid £10 to give lessons to pupils. This was the first time I had been back into a school since I had been a pupil. It was a really tough school and some of the pupils clearly had big problems, but I absolutely loved going in. It was the highlight of my week. This also triggered my early interest in working in schools.

Window of opportunity

I was now managing to scrape together money to live off by doing office jobs. I got a role selling double-glazing over the phone for a window company. It was all target based. I didn't mind ringing people as they couldn't see me. I used to get such a buzz when I managed to get an appointment for a consultant to do a home visit. It was also a stressful environment so we used to play jokes on each other and put on silly voices to customers. I was eventually sacked because I asked for some time off to play drums at a wedding at church. The team leader said, "If you don't come in for your shift on Saturday you are sacked."

I went to the wedding as I had already committed to it and when I turned up later for my shift, they turned me away. I had no money so ended up walking home which was about five miles. I was swearing and cursing the whole way – I hadn't quite learnt about grace and forgiveness in those days.

Ivy Cottage, the church that I attended, was launching something new, it was called the 'New Life Team' and it was going to be a year out placement that involved evangelism training and discipleship. As I was heavily involved in the youth work I decided this would be a good thing for me to aim for. After chatting and praying with some wise people I applied and was accepted. We all had part time jobs, and did the 'New Life Team' for the rest of the week. We would meet in the cellar of Ivy Manchester and did lots of Bible study, had discussions and also spent time developing as a team.

The ultimate aim of the year out was to help develop us as Christians and see if we had any type of calling towards full time Christian work. For me it was an ideal time to test and work through my new found faith. I also had lots of questions and some of these were answered during my time on the team. We often led events at other churches and youth groups. I was asked to drum at a lot of these and also helped plan and lead various activities. I grew massively both as a person and a Christian over that year. We even visited Turkey and worked alongside a missionary who lived there who had links with the church.

The time I have just mentioned was seminal for me. It was the start of God grounding me in the Bible, helping me understand more of His plans for me and His love for the world. My confidence was growing and my questions and my hurts were being dealt with. I was changing and maturing for a purpose. I knew true friendship and felt loved and accepted for who I was. My skills were praised and encouraged: I had found a place where I was needed and useful. I began to think differently about myself and my future. My dreams began to widen as I started to realise that God was most definitely on my case.

I did not know it at the time, but God was planting the ideas and the heart in me to run my own mission one day and to be something of a rescuer myself. People like me were going to hear about this God and come face to face with how He could change them. All through me.

But lots more had to happen first.

CHAPTER 4

How God shaped me

"There is no greater discovery than seeing God as the author of your destiny".

Ravi Zacharius

Lacking confidence, and sometimes struggling with overpowering shyness, life was not always easy. But even at this time I had the sense that God was preparing me for greater things.

I started working in a voluntary capacity for Trafford Youth For Christ, spending my days helping to plan lessons and assemblies. We also ran activity weeks, at the end of which we presented the Gospel and many young people gave their lives to Christ. This is where it finally clicked with me that I too was called to share Jesus with others. It helped me start to grow in my faith and maturity.

For the first time in my life I was truly beginning to develop as a Christian and get a solid Biblical grounding. At this time I met a wonderful guy called Phil Allen who was the new boss of Trafford Youth For Christ. We went on to be great friends. Little did he know that he would be the catalyst leading me into a future role!

South Africa

Around this time I went to a gig in Liverpool to watch a band called 'Iona'. I was really into their music and the drummer was one of the best Christian musicians in the country. After the gig I saw a poster advertising another event by a group called 'The Continentals Choir'. The advert promised that lots of young people from all over the country would be performing, and that at the end of the concert they would be auditioning for a tour to South

Africa. A few weeks later we returned to the church in Liverpool for this concert. It was amazing and I really loved all the songs they played. At the end, I found myself going forward to audition as drummer. I played for a couple of minutes. I was told I was good enough and encouraged to apply. I did and my application was successful. Somehow I got onto the tour but I had to raise £1500 in sponsorship money first.

This was 1995 and £1500 was a huge sum to me as I had nothing. So I did a sponsored 24-hour-drum in my bedroom (which made me less than popular with my housemates). At the time I was living in a shared house in Northenden with a load of guys from church. Through generous gifts from the people at church I raised enough money to go.

The tour started with a week's rehearsal camp in Northampton. Here I met the 30 or so other young people who had been picked to go on the tour. We rehearsed the songs and then went around churches all over the UK. We were hosted by families in each church we performed in. Whilst I struggled with this constant change for a fortnight, it helped my confidence grow. It forced me to be more vocal and helped develop me.

I had started to work out that the more I pushed myself into positive things and allowed myself to be stretched, the more I learnt about God and the more I trusted His plans for me. That was a realisation that began to change my perception of myself, and my dreams. After two weeks touring in the UK we set off for South Africa. This was only my second time abroad and I remember feeling quite anxious and wondering how I had ended up at Heathrow airport with a bunch of Christians and an electric drum kit packed into some large bags.

After arriving in South Africa we stayed in a motel for the first night. We then took the long drive to Durban. We travelled everywhere by mini coach and I soon learnt that I would need to get used to these long, uncomfortable and boring journeys.

We arrived at the first church we were due to play at. I took the bags containing the drum kit and started to unload them. I quickly realised something was not right. All the bars that the drums sat on were bent. The power supply was in bits with wires hanging from it. We showed it to our hosts at the church. They scratched their heads for a while. Soon someone arrived and took away the power supply. A little while later they came back with it all taped together. It looked like a bomb. Nervously, I plugged it in, expecting sparks and a big bang but it worked and the show went on.

It was not until I started writing this book that I made the parallel in my mind that this is what has happened with my life. Time and time again things should not have worked out for me. Things should have ended with a big bang and yet the show went on. God has been in control and has made some incredible things out of an unpromising start.

This short trip literally changed my worldview. We visited many townships and I remember feeling shocked that people had to live in such poverty. The sight of rows of squalid huts held together with old corrugated iron and rubbish imprinted itself on my brain. It reinforced how lucky I was to have all that I had. I was struck by the smell and the lost look in the eyes of people who passed you. "How was it right that this happened in the world?" I wondered. "How could I have been given so much and they so little?"

I had many questions.

We moved around all over South Africa playing at all sorts of churches with audiences ranging from 100 people up to 1000 plus and we ended the tour in Cape Town. It was the usual custom for us to stand on the stage at the end of the concert and wait to be allocated our host family for the night. One particular night something was up. The leaders of the tour were locked in deep conversation with the church leaders. The family who had been due to host me did not want to take me. They did not want me because I was black. I was so shocked.

They were a white family and were unhappy to host a black lad. This may have been more to do with what their neighbours may have thought, I don't know. But I was very offended. It gave me a first-hand glimpse of the challenges people faced there on a daily basis.

I ended up swapping with another team member. When I turned up at my host's house I found it was like a palace. Later, I asked the person who I had been swapped with what their house was like and they had ended up in a house like a 'shoe box'. God had blessed me for the disgrace and shame of the situation. He had given me double for my trouble and showed me what He thought of the colour of my skin!

I cannot really stress enough how much this event and the whole of my time in South Africa changed my life. It gave me a new sense of purpose. It drew me closer to God. It showed me what was possible when Christians, of all creeds and colours, worked together. I loved getting to know the other people we toured with. I even went out with a girl for a few weeks after it ended. I was offered another tour to the States soon afterwards but decided against it due to lack of money.

Unemployed again

After the tour I got a role as a temporary Customer Service Advisor at a Job Centre. It was a ridiculous 'temp' role on a three-month contract. After three months they would fire me, send me home for a week then re-employ me. Everyone I ever spoke to about this agreed that surely the Job Centre should be setting a better example! I stuck at this for a while then got into a sales role that was more interesting. I worked for an industrial supplies company. Eventually, they gave me a company car. As he handed me the keys, the Sales Director quipped, "If you crash it Christie, I'll sack you ********"!

The next day, after a brief discussion, I was promptly fired for backing it into a wall. In my defence the wall was at the garage where I was clearing out and cleaning the car. It was a low wall. What can I say?

Meeting Jo

In 1996 Ivy Cottage Church planned a joint youth service with Emmanuel Church down the road. I was asked to play the drums for the evening. The band was a mixture of Ivy and Emmanuel people. One of the girls singing that night was called Jo. I remember thinking she was very pretty but of course I was far too shy to say anything. Being a smart lad I knew that if I said something in front of another excitable girl, they would promptly run off and tell her. Within seconds one such excitable member of the band had run over and told Jo I liked her.

Jo and I started chatting after the service and every time we did any joint events, I would always make sure I helped with whatever she was involved in. After a few weeks I plucked up the courage to ask her if she wanted to go out for a drink. She agreed and we met in a pub a couple of days later. There was something very different about her and I realised I really liked her.

We instantly hit it off and I was pleased she seemed to like and accept me too. We started meeting up more regularly and one day I asked her out properly. She said yes! Things continued to look up for me. Jo and I got on so well; she was really sincere and I always knew where I stood with her. One day it occurred to me that I really loved this girl. This was an enormous realisation for me. Remember that I didn't find it easy to express my emotions, and had found it very hard to understand love and those deep feelings that come with it. Meeting Jo made me realise how much God had healed me. I was in a normal loving relationship for the first time. I loved someone and I was about to tell her!

On your bike!

To my relief, Jo felt the same about me. NICE ONE! I was now much more settled. But I was also still capable of doing some quite silly things. As I had no car Jo used to lend me her bike to get home to Northenden. I think her parents had bought her this. One day I came out of her flat to find the u-lock still attached to the railings but the bike missing. After searching around the grounds we realised someone must have stolen it. I had obviously forgotten to thread the lock through the bike properly and just fixed it around the quick release seat post! Jo was less than impressed and it meant I had to walk everywhere for a while! Whoops!

At this time, mobile phones were just starting to catch on. I decided I needed one, as I was a total gadget freak. None of my friends had a phone so I didn't really have anyone to speak to on it. It was quite pointless me owning one! I was on a pricey monthly contract but told Jo I was borrowing it as I was too embarrassed to tell her it was mine. I really could not afford it and after a threatening letter from the phone company I had to go cap-in-hand to Dad to borrow the money to buy out the contract.

Jo and I had a lot of fun, and there were a couple of adventurous holidays too, though not in the traditional sense. Nothing was ever straightforward when I was around.

Once we took a National Express coach to Dorset. It seemed to stop at every town, village and lamppost between Manchester and Dorset. It took hours on a steaming hot day. When we got to the campsite, frazzled and grumpy, we started to pitch the small tent we had borrowed. Basically it was no bigger than a kid's toy tent. It was the tiniest most miniature one we had ever seen! At night we had to stack all our possessions up against the zipped up door. I am blessed with a micro bladder so imagine how annoying it was to shift everything in the middle of the night to go out to the loo. When it rained, everything got soaked. Jo just took it all in her stride though. I think she even managed to find it funny.

Cars and sheep

We had another break where some friends very kindly lent us a car. We went to Barmouth in Wales for a week. We had very little money at this stage so a car was a real luxury. Well, it was, until it broke down. We somehow managed to get it to a garage. The car was pretty much dead and so the car's owner told us to leave it in Wales and get a bus to Chester, then a train home. He would return the following weekend to sort the car out.

Jo's parents lived in North Wales but were away for the weekend, otherwise a simple phone call would have resulted in them rescuing us.

We needed cash for the bus but none of the local cash points were working! The next nearest bank with a cash point was a ten mile round trip – it was a Sunday so none of the banks were actually open. The kind garage owner lent us 2 bikes so we set off on those. I had no idea how unfit we both were. Jo lasted about 2 miles on steep Welsh roads but then she stopped and declared that she was not going any further. She happened to say this at an obligingly-placed pub. She stayed there whilst I cycled on doing the remaining miles alone. I managed to find the bank and gratefully put my card in to withdraw the cash.

I got back to a rested Jo and we returned to the garage to hand back the bikes. We then enjoyed a long hot bus journey across Wales to Chester, followed by a few hours waiting at Chester station and finally a train journey back to Manchester.

The next day Jo rang her parents to tell them about our 'adventure'. Jo's mum asked why we hadn't just phoned them to come and pick us up. It turned out they weren't away at all – Jo had the weekends mixed up. We saw the funny side – eventually.

Getting serious

Jo and I did everything together now and I got on well with Austin, the boyfriend of one of her housemates, Sarah. He had a strong faith and we used to go for beers and chat stuff through. He really helped me to realise again how much God had planned for me. It was at this point that I started to realise that I needed to really start to read the Bible, grow in my faith and attempt to listen to what God wanted to do in my life. I soon realised that part of that plan was to propose to Jo.

I asked her Dad and to my relief he agreed to my suggestion! In the summer of 1998 I proposed and Jo instantly said, "Yes"! We spent the next part of the year excitedly planning the wedding and in the July of 1999 we got married. It was the most incredible day with all of our friends and family gathered together. It was such a celebration! I knew my mum and dad were thrilled. They had stuck with me through really rough times when all of us doubted that anything good was going to come of Christie Spurling. Now I had landed a stunning Christian woman as my bride. I couldn't stop smiling. God had been very good to me.

Bible College

Just before we got married, and after a lot of discussion with Jo, I felt that I should do some kind of youth work qualification. I looked at various options and after much prayer I decided to approach the Nazarene Theological College in Didsbury, Manchester - just around the corner from our church. I went to an open day for a look around. I think I also had a semi-formal conversation with some of the academics. I had one stumbling block to getting in: I had no qualifications. I had a fair bit of youth work experience by now but nothing on paper. Not even one GCSE to my name. They asked if I would be willing to sit an entrance test and so I went back another day and did this. I can't remember what it entailed, but I did enough to pass.

Rather unbelievably for someone like me, I found myself studying for the Oasis Youth Ministry Course. Part of the week was spent in lectures; the other half was on placement at Altrincham Methodist Church in Cheshire - 10 minutes from where I grew up in Lymm.

The provision of God at this time was amazing. There was a flat above the church that Jo and I could live in, rent-free. So we started our married life above a church coffee shop. We said goodbye to our friends at Ivy Cottage as Altrincham Methodist would be our home church for a while. On the first or second day at college the Principal called me into his office. I remember having a sinking feeling like I had had so many times before when I had been summoned to see the headteacher as a youth. He sat me down and asked me to consider taking my earring out. His reason was that some students from other places in the world may view me wearing it as a sign that I was gay. I duly took it out. I then went home, put it straight back in and nothing was said about it again.

I studied hard but still really struggled with the workload, but I made some good friends on the course and that helped me along. Because I was happy, fulfilled and enjoying myself, my behaviour was good in the lectures. I really battled whenever we had tests or exams but I stuck with it. It was the modules about youth work that I tended to score more highly in, rather than the theology-based ones. In my mind it was the youth work that interested me. I was always very last minute with deadlines and could often be found hunched over my computer at 3am.

Whilst at Altrincham I was tasked with running the youth work and was line-managed by the minister. It was sometimes a challenge because the church wanted a great deal from me in the limited hours I could give, due to college work. I made some amazing friends whilst there, many of whom I am still in contact with now. Doing the course was really tough at times and I wanted to quit on several occasions but I knew that I had responsibilities now, as a married man, so decided that I couldn't just walk out on this. I had to stick it out.

I set up some youth groups and we were getting good numbers. We did some youth services and I ran a weekly young peoples' home group in our flat. I was still smoking at this time so had to keep sneaking off to avoid being seen but I'm sure people knew. I passed the course and started looking for youth work jobs around the country.

I focussed on looking into church-based youth work; this was despite a niggling feeling that I felt more called to work with young people who would not darken the doors of a church.

But I did not feel right in myself and was not doing well at interviews. We left Altrincham Methodist Church and moved into a flat in Sale. I had passed my diploma and should have been happy, but something wasn't right deep down. Not getting a church-based job after all my hard work really affected me. I ended up taking a job in the factory at the offices where Jo worked. I found it hard that after all that study and hard work here I was working as a warehouse operative. I felt very low.

One day Jo turned to me and gently said, "Christie, I think you should see a doctor as you seem incredibly down."

I agreed to go to the GP and explained how I was feeling. The doctor instantly diagnosed me with clinical depression and put me on some tablets. This was to be my first, but not my only, bout of depression. I had to learn to manage it.

I continued to work in the warehouse picking orders of bed sheets and boxing them up, tidying up and doing anything else I was asked to do. The guys who worked there were a good laugh and I got on well with them. It was in that warehouse, halfway up some steps, picking orders that I heard about the 9:11 terror attacks. We all worked on in shock and waited to get home to see those terrifying images.

I missed being with young people. I questioned why God had let me get on the course and pass it and then had not provided me with a youth work job. I felt very low in myself and found those months hard.

Back into care

One day, Jo saw an advert for a job as a Residential Social Worker at a local home for young people. It was the same sort of place as Hilltop. I applied and got an interview. The only down side to the role was that it was shift work, but I felt I could cope with this as it was with young people again and I needed the experience. I started work at the Didsbury School. It took young people from all over the UK with severe EBD (Emotional and Behavioural Disorders). I was quickly trained up by the managers, Maureen and Andrea, and started off working in a small house they had in Longsight, Manchester. We cared for a couple of young people and basically made sure they were well looked after. They frequently absconded, were arrested and fought us off. You name it, it happened.

Soon after starting I was told I would be working at the main home which slept about 15 young people. It was a very old and tired building. The young people we cared for were always extremely volatile and we spent our lives constantly breaking up fights, clearing up smashed rooms, being spat on and assaulted. I loved it! You might think that is strange, but I could relate to their behaviour and their language. It was not alien to me, nor did it faze me as it might with other people not used to it. I was really good with these kids because I 'got' them. They respected me and listened to me - well, sometimes anyway!

I pretty much saw the worst of the worst possible behaviour you could imagine on an almost daily basis. These kids were all really broken. As a Christian I felt I wanted to help them. I used to offer to take them away on holidays to get them out of the volatile environment. I was at my happiest in this role when I could get them off site. I used to just grab the car and take them for drives around Manchester and stop for chips on the way home. One lad used to ask me to take him around the city centre. Once he instructed me to drive near Piccadilly train station. He then proceeded to open the window and shout out at all the prostitutes, "How much, love?"

I quickly put a stop to driving around there.

On another occasion I was driving down the motorway with a minibus full of rather grumpy young people. An argument erupted and one of them opened the door and threatened to jump out as I drove at 70mph. I had to pull over on the hard shoulder and break up the fight. I quickly learnt about how to defuse these situations, often using humour. These kids were acting in exactly the same way I had done at Hilltop. I empathised with them as I had been in the same environment.

It wasn't all bad. There were moments of real fun and laughter. Some of the kids we were looking after came from the most shocking backgrounds and I felt sorry for them. Just like my adopted mum had felt sorry for all those kids in the children's home she had worked in.

I did this job for a while and learnt a great deal. I was now being asked to be an acting team leader, but I was going for promotion interviews and being unsuccessful. It felt like I was trusted enough to do team leading but that they didn't want to pay me for the role. I was also getting fed up of doing constant shift work, especially working nights.

Moving on again

I went for a pint with Phil Allen one evening and he mentioned that Trafford Borough Council was looking for Behaviour Support Workers. He gave me some contact details and I went and spoke to a couple of people about the role. I decided to apply, had an interview and was taken on. I was assigned pupils who were incredibly challenging. I followed them around the school and supported them in lessons, helping to manage their behaviour. I tried to keep them out of trouble and spent lots of time chatting to them and trying to get them to think about the consequences of their actions. It was a strange position to be in because I had hated school but here I was, back in one again, actually helping pupils to do school work and access their education.

I met some great teachers in the job, some who had been working hard for thirty years and knew just how to get the best out of their more difficult kids. Where I found examples of good teaching I would soak up all the tips I could and ask lots of questions. God was setting me up for the work I would start later. I did not know this at the time, but still felt keen to learn all I could to improve at my role. In one of the schools they gave me a 'walkie-talkie.' and I loved it. I felt like some kind of a detective! I used to wander around tracking down missing pupils. Phil worked at the school too and when he had his radio on we would chat away to each other all day.

After a few months the council noticed I was good with the pupils and moved me around to lots of different schools to work with the neediest and most challenging ones. So here I was again, faced with the challenge of constant change, , but looking back it was a good way of getting a real insight into the education system in Trafford.

Breaking news

After doing this role for nearly two years I got a call one day asking me to attend a meeting at the town hall. I went, and was told the news that would go on to totally change the shape of my future. Looking back, the meeting was a really pivotal point in my journey. I now realise that God had bought me to that stage for a reason and that all the youth-related roles at the schools and churches I'd worked in had been leading to this.

I turned up to this meeting and two ladies from the council's HR team were waiting for me. One of them was attractive and friendly. The other looked like she was chewing a wasp's nest. I had heard rumours about what was being proposed but this was the first time it was confirmed. They told me that Trafford schools would now be directly responsible for hiring Behaviour Support Workers. If you currently worked in a school you might be offered a role there but there were 'catches'. All the new roles were paid for term time only. I was on a fairly low salary anyway, so this would mean a significant drop in income. If you didn't want to do this, the options were redundancy or redeployment. There was nothing else available at the time in children's or youth services so I think they tried to offer me a role in the ticket office of a theatre, or in gardening and leisure. I was told by the 'wasp chewer' to take a couple of weeks to think about it. They ended the discussion by telling me that for some reason I was not entitled to any redundancy pay.

I took redundancy. I realised that I was not going to get any money, but I wanted out of this unreliable system.

By now Jo was heavily pregnant with our first child. I had been to the first scan and seen that picture of my child for the first time. As we walked back to the car I took out a cigarette and proceeded to smoke it. I felt really challenged to stop. It seemed hypocritical seeing that new life and then smoking something that could, in time, kill me. So over the next few weeks I gradually quit. Whenever I struggled with the cravings I had a mental image in my head of the scan photo and that kept me on the right track. Losing my job just before our baby was due wasn't ideal, but we felt God would provide for us.

Amy Faith burst into the world on the 4th of October 2004. I had nine months to get used to the idea of being a dad for the first time but nothing really prepares you. I was as helpful as I could be to Jo as she was in labour but I did have to leave the room as she had an epidural (a fainting father is no use to anyone)! Something else struck me that had been playing on my mind for months. Amy was the first blood relative I had ever met. For this reason she was, and still is, so precious to me. I loved having a baby. We adapted to life with the three of us and our church family was really supportive. Amy was not a huge fan of sleeping as a baby but we got through it!

As there were no jobs available in my skill area, I took a low-paid driving job delivering vehicles around the UK. Surprisingly I loved it, as I enjoy driving so much. There was plenty of thinking time driving around alone all day and God used those few months to get my thoughts in line with His. I did some crazy journeys and was up and down the country all day every day. I remember being stitched up once and being made to drive a milk truck all the way from Lands End to Barnsley, limited to forty miles an hour. When I got to the depot everyone was in hysterics. I laughed as well - eventually. Whilst travelling around the country in a minibus I sat with my PDA (an electronic notebook) and wrote plans for my next idea. God was whispering some ideas to me and for the first time in my life I was not only ready to listen, I also saw myself as someone up for the challenge.

CHAPTER 5

The journey towards 'N-Gage'

It was now 2004. I was still involved in youth work at Ivy Cottage. Whilst I loved working with this group, I felt a real God-given desire to work with the kind of young people who might never have felt they were welcome in church. I wanted to find out where the local young people hung out and what their needs were. So, over a few weeks, I drove around on Friday evenings to find where they were meeting up and what they were doing. I noticed large numbers were gathering in Didsbury Park, getting up to no good, being loud, and committing minor crimes. After a few trips to observe their behaviour, I decided to get a small team to go there with me, chat to these young people, befriend them, and see what we could do to help them find positive outlets for their energies and time.

I was given the chance to say a few words in a church service and a number of people came forward to offer to volunteer to be part of the team. I decided that it would be a good idea to speak to the police about what we were planning so I made an appointment with an officer at Didsbury Police Station. As I told him who I was and what I wanted to do, he simply stared back at me. I don't think many people were offering help to the police at that time.

I told him that I had noticed lots of young people in Didsbury Park on a Friday and Saturday night and that, as someone involved in youth work at a local church, I wanted to start going out and helping them. When I explained that we would be doing this voluntarily, he almost had to pick his jaw up from the floor. He was incredibly surprised and grateful that we were even interested in *attempting* to do something about this situation.

He proceeded to explain that they were getting a lot of complaints and call-outs from residents living near Didsbury Park. Young people's bad behaviour was escalating and local homeowners were getting anxious about their property being targeted. Anything that we could do to help reduce the growing number of crime reports would be appreciated.

A new 'Shift'

So, with a small team of volunteers, we started weekly visits to Didsbury Park. We were quickly able to start conversations with the young people hanging around. We chatted to them, initially to find out what we could do to help keep them occupied and out of trouble. They suggested we got some sports gear as they liked playing football. So we went and bought a few balls and a rounders set. It was easy to get the young people to join in with us.

After trialling this for a few weeks I went back to the police and asked how they felt things were going. They told me that in the weeks we had been there they had had no complaints from anyone and no reported youth crime in the area. Something was working! They asked me to carry on running the teams as it really was helping to reduce boredom and crime. So we carried on visiting the park and working with the young people gathered there. The teams grew as more Ivy Cottage people began to get involved.

We called the work we were doing 'Shift'. The idea behind this was that everyone else was expecting the young people to be moved on by the police, (being told to 'shift'), but we were encouraging them to stay and engage with us. I recall someone taking a picture of my friend Dave Lamberth and myself walking through the park with a baseball bat! Far from being menacing and dangerous, we were giving those young people the opportunity to change their stories and use a baseball bat for its intended purpose!

Boxers and Barbeques

We really got to know those young people. They respected and valued us for coming out and engaging with them. They often said that they felt it was a good thing for people from a local church to volunteer in this way. We now had a small team of people from church, including a man named Bobbi-Joe Edwards.

Bobbi-Joe was a boxer. He was brilliant with the young people. One Friday night the park was full of kids and we were chatting with them and playing footy. Bobbi-Joe arrived carrying a large bag. He then proceeded to take out some boxers' skipping ropes. I had no idea what he was planning to do. But then he started doing that really fast skipping, where the ropes whirr around, like 'Rocky' in the film. Within seconds he had a crowd of young people around him, all wanting a turn. The lads felt they could do it faster than him so they all had a try at skipping and it kept them engaged for hours. One night we did a barbecue for them, again the young people were really chuffed and seemed to really appreciate what we had done. I later found out I needed permission for the barbecue from the council. Oops, never mind!

Activities like this were a great way for Christians to be out in the local area engaging with young people who were at risk of becoming involved in anti-social behaviour. As we chatted to the kids, we told them about our lives and naturally shared our faith. We encouraged them and I believe we were really helping these young people that others were finding so hard to reach. I remember one week one of the team was having a chat with a group of lads and the subject had got onto relationships. In a very normal way he gave this golden nugget of advice: "If you don't feel ready to have a baby, don't be having sex". This kind of informal but helpful and life-steering conversation was a key part of what we were doing. I could tell that many of the lads took on board what he had said. The police continued to be supportive and seemed happy with our work.

Jumping off the cliff

In 2005 Jo and I found ourselves increasingly talking about my future. I felt that there was a possibility that God was calling me to do this kind of work more efficiently and professionally. We were praying a lot about whether I should leave my driving job and concentrate on this instead.

On occasions, God really speaks to me through dreams and one night I had a really vivid and descriptive one: I was standing on a high mountain ledge and below me I could see a cityscape. God was telling me to look closely at the view. Then I felt God asking me to leap. I was arguing back and saying, "I'm not jumping! I'm not jumping!" My voice sounded deep, hoarse and tense, like Mr T from the A-Team!   God was asking me to take a leap of faith. Eventually I leapt off the precipice and, as I jumped, a huge gust of wind swept underneath me and carried me. As I soared above the city I could see lots of people, of all types, but mainly young people who needed help. God was showing me His children – those that society had forgotten or branded as hopeless. God was showing me how He felt about those kids and how He wanted me to have His heart for them. That dream was incredibly significant for me. It showed me that I needed to step into the unknown.

After a bit more prayer and discussion with Jo and with a group of friends from church I felt it was time for me to leave my driving job. So I did just that. I walked away from my secure salary with a mortgage and a car to pay for, as well as a new baby in the family. But I was at peace. I had no doubt in my mind. This was what God was asking me to do.

Step Up

In March 2005 I worked from home for a few weeks writing a new School Inclusion Programme. I called it *'Step Up'*. It was amazing how much knowledge God had given me from the various roles I had worked in, and also my own experience of exclusion and behavioural problems at school. The course seemed to come very naturally to me. I had taken many notes over the years and knew where the gaps in young people's education were. I felt lots of young people were knocked down by society and I wanted to encourage them to stand tall and believe they could achieve something purposeful. The image we used on our first brochure was of a rock climber. The material and this image were telling kids what I thought of them and their potential. YOU CAN AIM HIGHER! *'Step Up'* had ten core activities and themes for young people to work through. They were:

1. Team Challenges 1: Various team games to get the group working well together.

2. Video Diaries: Each pupil to record a video diary about their life.

3. Prison Awareness 1: A look at the reality of life in prison.

4. Drugs Education 1: The risks and potential criminality of drug taking.

5. Team Challenges 2: Building on week 1, with different, more challenging activities.

6. Looking Ahead: the reality of life on benefits; the positives of getting a job.

7. Citizenship/Law and Order: being a positive citizen; observing laws.

8. Drugs Education 2: a more detailed look at drugs and the associated risks.

9. Prison Awareness 2: a more detailed look at a DVD about a prisoner.

10. Reward/Evaluation: course evaluation with the group and feedback on success.

I worked on the sessions for a while, buying DVDs about subjects like prison and drugs to help in my research. I got a few people to read through the course to check it over for me. All these people had a good eye for detail and in different ways brought order and structure to my ideas.

Trialling the course

So finally the *'Step Up'* course was ready and I needed to trial it. I sent a letter to a few tough schools asking them to consider running a pilot. Brookway High School - now Manchester Health Academy - got in touch and invited me in for a meeting.

They gave me eight difficult lads to test my material on. After sorting out paperwork, getting approval from the Headteacher and completing a police check, I went in once a week for ten weeks and delivered a two-hour session. For the drug awareness lessons I joined forces with an organisation called 'Eclypse' and they delivered the two drug sessions in partnership with me. The group was really, really tough. All the lads had all sorts of issues going on, both in and out of school. But we stuck with it.

Teachers came in occasionally to check on the progress but most of the time I was allowed to get on with the programme on my own. I discovered this was vital if I wanted the pupils to open up. They needed to trust me and get to know me and after a few sessions I noticed behaviour improving. It didn't take me half an hour to start the lessons anymore. I made the group times as interactive as possible. I left time to discuss questions and I was clear about my expectations of their behaviour. Attendance was an issue at times but as the course progressed, it got better. They responded to questions and opened up about their lives. The sessions that really seemed to work amazingly well were the team building, prison and drug sessions. These are still the key sessions that we deliver today, albeit in a slightly different format.

I wanted to get these lads to think about the consequences of their actions; to see that without an education life would be harder for them. I wanted to show them that they had a choice. I wanted to show them who they could be. I wanted to show them that I cared.

I was deeply aware that I was a positive male role model for these guys. Many of them had no-one in their lives influencing them for good. This was one reason that I did the course but it was so much more than that. Slowly, these hardened, bitter young people softened. They let me into their worlds, their fears and their pain. I think it was genuinely life-changing material for them.

I learnt lots about how to manage the sessions in those early days. I also made notes about what did and did not work. At the end of the course we discussed all the feedback we had been given by the pupils. We looked at ways we could improve the sessions and discussed the way forward. After the evaluations we finished working in that school, but I never forgot that first bunch of kids. Their stories and their problems convinced me that there were many more young people who needed reaching.

I began talking to some other schools about running 'Step Up'. Gradually I started getting more bookings. It became exciting to be involved in more young people's lives at such a time of critical decision making for them: "Will I take drugs?" "Will I sell drugs?" "Will I end up like my dad, or my uncle?"

I was trying to show them that they had a choice, that they had the power to shout a loud "No!" and aim for higher, better things. And it was starting to impact their lives. I could see their opinions of themselves changing in front of my eyes. At times, it was very moving.

Registering the charity

By now we had a Board of Trustees and had started to register as a charity, called 'N-Gage'. My trustees were an amazing team. Jo and I worked on the registration process and we started having regular trustee meetings. At this stage I knew very little about charitable processes and it was a very steep learning curve for me. We set up a bank account and in 2007 we were accepted and registered with the Charity Commission. It was a relief and also a responsibility. It was official! I was now doing the very last thing any of my school teachers would ever have expected. I was helping other disaffected children access school and an education!

New office

As a couple we decided I needed somewhere to be based. Working from home was less than ideal and I was starting to accumulate a lot of resources that I used for the sessions. What I needed most was space to store everything. Another charity was just starting at Ivy called 'Dignity,' run by a guy called Jon Witt. After a discussion one day we decided to find offices together as this was the most cost effective way for us both to move forward. So we eventually moved in to an office at the top of an old mill in Stockport. It was a big space but the lift up to it was a bit shaky and broke frequently.

By this stage I had about £6,000 coming in each year from gifts, fundraising events and people making monthly donations. This was used to pay me a small salary and went towards the office rent. People really caught the vision for what I wanted to achieve. We decided the strap line for 'N-Gage' would be 'Helping unlock young people's potential'. It has been this ever since!

After a few months based in Stockport we moved to a new office at Emmanuel Church in Didsbury. Most of the work we did was in South Manchester so it made sense for me to be based there, rather than

Stockport. I continued to go into schools and deliver the sessions and in the evenings the team would go out and deliver the 'Shift' detached work. We were still really valued by Greater Manchester Police and they took an active interest in what we were doing.

'Safe' spaces

Our church had started meeting in a Secondary school in Wythenshawe called Parklands. I made an appointment to see the new Headteacher there and he liked what we offered. He gave us some of his most challenging pupils. I worked with a group of lads each week in a unit attached to the school. These were pupils who were really disengaged, despairing and dangerous.

I found it incredibly tough getting them to sit and do anything so I quickly had to learn lots of strategies for dealing with their behaviour. One thing I noticed was that if you spoke their language it broke down barriers. So I used to speak back at them using their words, like "safe, mate" and "that kid is ill". I also sometimes copied the young people's mannerisms, so with this group when a peer came into the room they would all clench fists and touch each other's fists. So I started doing this when I arrived. I would walk around the room and touch each young person's fist and say "Safe". Looking back at this from a spiritual point of view, perhaps God was doing the very same thing: using my hands to touch theirs and remind them that this was indeed a 'safe space' for them.

I soon started to realise that if I tried to copy their little habits it became quicker for them to accept me. On occasions if a young person was kicking off with me, I would copy them as if to say, "Yeah mate! I can do that too!" It often worked as it shocked the kids into silence or at least made them laugh!

One day, some pupils said something that made me really sad and determined to grow 'N-Gage' and help more young people. We were doing a session on getting a job. I went round the group and asked them what their dream job was. I got a range of responses including this: "I want to be the biggest drug dealer in Wythenshawe, like my brother."

What a life goal to have!! He wasn't joking either; he was looking to inherit the family business when his brother was locked up. To sit in a session and hear a 14-year-old say this shocked me. It wasn't his fault. This was the world he was being encouraged to operate in, but it broke my heart to hear it. Imagine if that was one of your children and that was all they felt they had to look forward to. Something in me rose up and I vowed that day that I would work my hardest to make sure that kids like him had other options.

Interestingly, not all the other lads in the group agreed with his career choice and some clearly stated this. We had a big discussion about drugs and the group told me that they felt working and getting a job was the best way forward for them. I think they agreed that because of the way they were acting at that time, getting something that would pay them would be a challenge.

I quickly realised that my testimony could have a massive impact in stopping a generation of people from making the same mistakes I had made at exactly the same age.

Ultimately a lot of the pupils I was getting referred to me were like I had been ten years earlier. But I could help them. I knew I could. I just needed more opportunities, more kids, more funding and more schools.

'Transform' is born

Caz, a friend from Ivy Church, was volunteering for N-Gage. She was working on a new project for us, running a day of community action for some of the pupils we were working with in Parklands High School. We spoke to a warden at Wythenshawe Park and asked if we could book a day to bring a load of young people to do some volunteer work in the park. The idea was they would do the park project and then be given some kind of reward. We decided to call it 'Transform' because we wanted to change an area and at the same time transform people's perception of Wythenshawe's young people. Caz and I went into the school and led an assembly about what we were planning. We had a few young people who said they would come. We went back to the park warden and confirmed we would be joining her for the day. She told us they had plenty of work that the young people could get involved in.

On the morning of the project we set up a small table in the park with our logo on it. And we waited. My biggest fear was simple: "What if no kids turn up?"

After what seemed like an age, slowly but surely a couple of young people started to arrive. Some I recognised from the groups I ran in school, others I had never seen. There was one lad who was always in lots of trouble at school and I was really praying he would come. I was delighted when I saw his face. I suspected that much of his behaviour was to mask a lack of confidence and I knew this day would certainly boost it.

The format of the day was simple enough. We would spend the morning doing tidying up jobs, provide lunch, do a bit more work then send the kids home. They would all get a certificate to put in their school 'Record of Achievement' to say they had completed the day successfully.

We started the morning work which involved clearing a path ready for some chipped bark to be laid. We had volunteers from church to support the young people and help as needed. I loved hearing all the conversations that were taking place. The volunteers were asking the young people why they had decided to do it and sharing about their faith with these kids. The park warden, Philippa, was brilliant. Keeping the work moving, she offered praise and supported us, giving advice when needed.

Again, it was really exciting to see my fellow Christians doing something meaningful with a load of kids for whom church seemed a distant place that wasn't relevant. I started to realise the impact of taking Christians out into communities and getting them to engage with these hardest-to-reach kids. The day was a great success. The park wardens loved us. The kids were all buzzing and a week or so later we took them all on a reward trip to Blackpool Pleasure Beach. We paid for half of each ticket price and their parents paid the rest. The kids had an amazing time. It was great to teach them the rewards of hard work and sticking to a commitment.

Around this time we made some links with Brownley Green Baptist Church in Wythenshawe. They had a big sports hall and wanted a mural painted on it so my wife Jo (an artist) designed a huge mural and some of the kids from the first 'Transform' group helped paint it. Members of the church fed us and again it was wonderful to watch tough kids meeting Jesus the only way they might ever meet Him, through these Christian people.

Things continued to grow and develop and I started to get more schools work. Many established schools seemed to be crying out for the additional support we offered for their challenging pupils. We were also doing lots of activities with a small group who I had met at Parklands High school. They did lots of community action projects with us and were a bit of a core group we focused our efforts on. We took a few to a big Christian event at the Apollo Theatre in Manchester. It was a much more evangelistic evening than I had expected and I had no idea how they would react. However, when the guy on the stage did an appeal at least three of the young people responded and put their hands up to commit their lives to Jesus. It was a really special moment for me and for 'N-Gage'.

For the following six weeks after that I ran a Youth Alpha group at Ivy for them. It was really challenging because people kept dropping out of the small group and eventually we only had a couple still coming. It was also hard because they lived a little way away from church and would not attend the youth work at the Didsbury building. I do believe that what we did with those guys really sowed some seeds and helped them through some difficult times they were having, but I guess we will never truly know what God was saying to them at that time.

Back to Lymm High School

Towards the middle of 2008 I got a grant from N.O.M.S. (The National Offender Management Service) to pay for me to deliver our prison lesson in schools to 500 pupils. As we already had links with lots of schools we delivered it to either small groups or classes in existing schools. I had been chatting to a friend who was Head of R.E. at Lymm High School - my old school. I made an appointment and went in to chat to a couple of Heads of Year. Who should be there but Mr Thomas, who had been my Head of Year when I was in school, and Mrs Lewis, who had really tried with me and had been so patient?

I explained a bit about what 'N-Gage did' and told them my story since leaving Lymm following the exclusion. They all seemed genuinely staggered that I, of all the pupils they had ever taught, had turned out the way I had, and was now sitting in a meeting trying to get back into school to talk to their pupils about prison (I had looked close to going there myself on occasions).

A few weeks later I returned to Lymm and did a day of prison lessons for about 100 pupils. At breaks and lunch times I went into the staff room and was surprised to see some more teachers who were still there from my time as a pupil. I remember sitting next to Mr Coleman, nervously drinking a coffee remembering how poorly I behaved for him, and also Mr Lawton. But everyone seemed thrilled at how I had turned out. After the day's session, which went really well, they asked if I could come in and work with a challenging group of pupils so I was booked for a ten week block. My friend was running a vocational centre in Broadoak High School in Partington. I had been in for a chat with him and he explained that he had a spare slot available. We took six lads from Lymm High School and did an eight-week motor mechanics course with them. It was great to watch these really tough lads grow and develop, learning new skills and new confidence.

I was starting to realise that the formula I was developing was useful in many settings and with many different types of kids. 'N-Gage' was working! It was transforming lives, giving kids a step up and changing the way they thought about themselves. My dream was becoming reality. God had blessed the leap from the clifftop more than I could have ever imagined. But there was more to come.

CHAPTER 6

The work grows on

"May the favour of the Lord our God rest on us; establish the work of our hands for us – yes, establish the work of our hands."

Psalm 90: 17

We continued to grow the work. I found that the strategy of offering to do a free 'taster session' prior to any booking worked well. Although the numbers weren't the be-all-and-end-all it was encouraging to see the work getting larger. In 2008 we delivered ten schools' work programmes in two secondary schools and two primary schools. We also led thirteen workshops to various youth and school groups, reaching a total of 250 young people. These included team-building sessions, drug awareness seminars and drum workshops. We delivered three 'Transform' community action projects with 30 participants. We worked with 125 young people doing our prison lesson in churches, schools and youth groups and we ran 8 detached 'Shift' sessions reaching 100 young people on the streets of South Manchester. The work was becoming established.

Taking on others

Most of the sessions were being delivered personally by me, meaning our work was not massively sustainable. I started to look around and see who I could draw in to come alongside me and help. As and when I could I would recruit volunteers from church to do certain projects with me, but I found that even this was not enough to keep the work growing effectively. I needed to get more regular assistance. We had two volunteers through church who offered to come into the office, taking on some of our administration tasks and helping us to start to pull together some more professional-looking publicity and logos.

Placements

We had also made links with Manchester University and Nazarene Theological College. I started taking students as part of their placement for youth work degrees. They came and learned about how a youth charity ran and at first I assumed that was all anyone would get out of it, but I soon realised that this was a great partnership on both sides. I found that I gained a lot from them too. They asked lots of questions and it really made me think about the methodology of what we were trying to do. It It made me much more effective in constantly questioning what we are doing and why.

Applications for Grants

We started to apply for grants to take on more staff as the work was growing much bigger than we could handle. We needed a lot of faith for this, as the credit crunch had started to hit and many organisations were cutting back. But God always came through for us. Soon a young lady called Rachel Gaunt came to work for us part time. She did an amazing job: putting systems in place to help organise the work and my time. She was really passionate about what we did and it eased the load on me to leave her to run things administratively. My dad was also planning to semi-retire. He had gained a wealth of experience setting up Cambridge Dial-a-Ride. He had a vast amount of knowledge about how to obtain funding so we took him on as a part-time Development Worker. His aim was to apply to larger grant makers so we could develop the work.

Breaking the bank

Interestingly, lots of banks seemed to be pro-actively giving grants away. We were put forward for £3000 from NatWest and people had to go into a branch to vote for us. Rachel was a whizz with social media and managed to whip up a bit of a storm and we won. I also had a very random email from a couple of lads who worked at Lehman's Bank. They were doing something called the 'Gumball Rally'. It was a crazy scheme that involved driving an old banger across Europe for charity. They had googled youth charities and bizarrely (because of the faithfulness of God!) had come across 'N-Gage'. So, after emailing me to see what we did, and taking a further look at our website, they chose us to raise funds for. I had never met them. They raised £500 for us which was matched by their employers, Lehman's, giving us £1000. A few days later I turned on the TV to see the memorable image of all the bank workers leaving the Lehman Brothers building in London, as the credit crunch began to take effect. I joked that perhaps it was that donation to 'N-Gage' that broke the bank! At that stage I had no idea of the extent of the crash. But it did make me wonder what had motivated the banks to suddenly have a hugely visible Corporate Social Responsibility. God saw to it that we benefitted and did not go without, which was great for the young people we were trying to reach.

Successes from failures

We now had a steady core of young people who were regularly coming and getting involved in our projects. One special group from Parklands High School really helped us shape the community action side of things. Jade, a girl who, by her own admission, was 'a real handful', started to get involved. I was also working with her in school. She was very close to exclusion. Everyone else saw her as a failure - but we didn't. I invested lots of time in her and she was a tough nut to crack, but we got there with her. Johnny was another of our 'regulars' and it was great to see him grow in confidence. He went on to university and Jade was recently accepted to train as a teacher. Stories like theirs constantly remind us why we do what we do!

We applied to the Joseph Rank Foundation for three years of funding. A man flew up from London to meet us. He asked lots of questions and we tried to answer as best as we could. He seemed impressed and a few weeks later we were awarded an amazing £30,000 over three years to develop 'N-Gage' even more!

Award-winning work

As our profile grew and the team increased we caught the attention of various agencies. In 2009 I won two awards for our work. The first came from Greater Manchester Police. Debra Green, who was running a charity called 'Citylinks', was holding a launch event at Wythenshawe Forum for a new project she was starting in Manchester. The Chief Constable of Greater Manchester Police was attending, along with quite a few other important people involved in community transformation. Debra had put me forward for an award. On the night I felt terrified. I was still petrified of public speaking and there were over 500 people in the room. My name was called and Sir Peter Fahy presented me with an award. My mum, dad and sisters were in the audience. I felt so proud that they saw me being rewarded for something positive. I hoped it went some way to making the challenging years more bearable. I said a few words about what I used to be like and how my life had changed and what I hoped to achieve by setting up 'N-Gage'. A local paper ran a story on me. It was greatly encouraging to find that our work was starting to be recognised and valued.

Changing the beat

I also won another award for a new project we had set up called 'The Beats'. I was working in Chorlton High School with some really tough pupils. They were a gang who used to rap and MC and were actually quite talented at it - once you stripped away all the swearing and gang references. Around this time my friend Andy was teaching at a school in Hale that was designated as a Specialist Technology College. He said that his school were due to give away some new laptops to another charity but there had been a problem and he asked if I would like them instead. It was amazing timing. I was very excited at the prospect of owning these for the young people to use.

A few days later six shiny, brand new computers arrived at our office. We bought some easy-to-use music creation software, loaded it up onto the laptops and took them into Chorlton High School. Over a number of weeks, with the help of an amazing teaching assistant there, we delivered the following:

- I showed a group of ten young people how to use the software.

- I told them that they had to create a few music tracks each.

- I gave the most challenging members of the group key roles. One was designated as the Producer, one was the Graphic Designer and another was the group Accountant. Finally, the last person was the Production Manager.

- I gave the group a budget and told them how long they had to make the tracks. They had to buy blank CDs, card and any other resources they would need. They then had to produce an EP album between them.

It was amazing to see how the young people responded. Watching those with allocated tasks trying to keep the group on track was sometimes amusing. As these were the more natural leaders of the group it was a good way of channelling their energy into something positive. The kids made their album, burnt their discs and created all the packaging.

Launch

I encouraged the kids to set up a stall one break time and asked people to make a donation for a copy of the CD. We raised £130 for charity. We chose an organisation that worked with young people of a similar age. My friend Lucy worked for a charity called 'Retrak' that worked with street children in Africa. The kids enjoyed the fact that they were helping people less fortunate than themselves.

We got the group to write a letter to some of Lucy's street kids asking them what they would like to do with the £130 we had raised. We had a reply back asking for football gear as they were all footy mad. So we got a lot of great sports equipment for them.

Then came phase two. I wondered how I was going to take a load of disaffected school-haters and get them to do an assembly to launch their album. I remember walking down the corridor on the way to the hall with them. All the pupils were groaning and saying that no one would buy the CD because it was 'macca' (or rubbish, to you and me). There was total disunity and disillusionment as they walked towards the assembly. Walking back up the corridor afterwards was a completely different story. There were group hugs, high fives, and surprised cries of "That was amazing!"

I'm telling you now that the change in the group was astounding. It had gone so well and for many of those young people, they had had their first taste of success as the result of their own creative ingenuity and legitimate hard work.

The headteacher of the school got us all in and congratulated us. A local paper ran a story on the project and I was nominated for a Manchester City Council 'Be Proud' award. I was invited to a swanky ceremony at the town hall. My parents came, as well as Jo and a number of others. I was not expecting to win. Gordon Burns, the BBC newsreader, was announcing the nominees. I was up against lots of other very deserving people and projects. But suddenly he said my name! I had won! In a daze I went up to collect my award. I was so proud, but the thing that filled me with the most joy was knowing what an incredible journey the Chorlton High School pupils had been on. It was a big step forward for them and for us as a charity.

More new team

By now it was 2010. The work continued to develop. School bookings were coming in thick and fast. I wondered whether it was time to take someone on to do more schools' work for us. Amazingly, at this time, we got a grant from Lloyds TSB to take on a youth and community worker. A lady called Rachel came and chatted to me one day after a service at church to tell me she was leaving her role in a band called TBC. She was interested in perhaps coming to work for us. I explained that we had some funding for a new role and that she should keep her eyes open for the advertisement. She applied and got the job.

One concern I had was making sure that whoever we appointed would be able to develop the work and get alongside the types of young people we were working with. I quickly realised I didn't need to worry with Rachel. Her whole approach and attitude to the kids was very similar to mine. She had a knack for knowing when to be strict, when to have a laugh and when she needed to let things go. It is very hard, if not impossible, to teach someone to be like that. You just need to have it in you. Rachel had just the right balance.

As part of her role she started to look after the 'Shift' detached work and our use of the youth bus that Greater Manchester Police now had. She planned events in the holidays as part of our 'Revolution' activity weeks. It was great that I was soon able to hand over responsibility for all our community-based work to her. She was full of ideas, a talented artist and had a real flair for anything creative. I loved having her around. She started to develop some new ideas and programmes for challenging young people. One such God-inspired idea was the very successful 'Young Leaders' initiative - something we still deliver now. She described it as a bit like an urban Duke of Edinburgh award scheme - without the camping! The police in particular really appreciated this programme and Rachel developed and delivered it to lots of tough young people. She went on to work for 'N-Gage' for three and a half years, proving to be a popular and well-liked member of staff. She was also great with external agencies as well as the countless young people she worked with and saw such potential in.

Leap of Faith

By now people were doing various fundraising activities for us such as marathons and other sponsored events. I felt I needed to rise to the challenge but what could I do? I hated running unless I was being chased by an authority figure - so I settled on a sky-dive. I wasn't great with heights and decided it was suitably scary! I went up in a tiny rubber-band-engine aircraft. Fear started to creep in.

I was strapped to a twenty stone ex-army guy (the only time I've ever been strapped to a bloke) and we were the second pair to leave the plane. The worst part is as you sit on the edge of the plane before you exit. Whoosh, and we were out. I have to say once the initial fear had passed I loved it. It was such an amazing feeling soaring in the clouds. As I was enjoying it so much the instructor did some crazy loops pulling ropes to make us soar left and right. Once on the ground I was buzzing. My parents and both sisters and their kids had come to watch. I did another jump a few years later from 15,000ft.

The big one

It was the 5th of December 2011. I was nervous. After a sleepless night it was D-day. I knew I had to pull all the stops out. It was a big day, certainly the biggest one so far for us as 'N-Gage'. After my normal school sessions I dashed back to the office, put a shirt on, hoping and praying that we would do ok. In the office I noted the biscuits and posh fizzy water. I said a hasty prayer along the lines of, "God I have no idea how I ended up here. I know I should have hoovered the carpet. Please help me to say the right thing and not burp because of the fizzy water. Amen!"

The doorbell rang but I didn't move. I heard people saying hello outside but nothing really registered. I was in some kind of stupefied daze. Then all four of them come into the room. I shook hands with each one, smiling as naturally as I could and anxiously trying to remember their names. My office quickly seemed very cramped but we all fitted in. Just.

They started asking questions and the next forty minutes or so sped by in a blur. I think my team and I did a good job of presenting what we do in an assertive way without being cocky. Andy Eadie, our Chairman, arrived late and was very apologetic. He was on great form however and had the right mix of being friendly and knowledgeable. His infectious passion for my work is impossible to explain but he understands it and wants everyone else to do the same. The way he describes what we do makes ME want to work for 'N-Gage'. Then I remember that I already do!

They fired questions at us and we all made a great job of answering. Half way through the meeting I started to relax. I was reminded of the Bible verse "If God is for us who can be against us?" (Romans 8:31) With this in mind I suddenly felt incredibly peaceful. I also had a fresh awareness that literally hundreds of people were praying for us.

The meeting ended and we ushered our guests out of our offices. I walked into our main office room where other staff was waiting to ask how it went. Unusually for me I said, "We did well, the best we could. Now we just have to hope and pray that we have done enough."

I walked back into my office and sunk into my chair, staring at the table around which we had all been sitting, only minutes before. I re-lived the meeting a few times and wondered what would happen if we were not chosen.

The meeting had been with four funders who were potentially offering us £50,000 over three years to fund a new schools worker. It was a mindboggling amount to be thinking about. The trust members that had come to interview us had selected four Manchester-based organisations to meet and would give the money to only one. Just to have been selected was an incredible boost for us. I felt like a lot was resting on me as the CEO to get this money. I knew what it would mean. The fund could enable us to take on another Schools' Worker so we could expand our reach. In a way that none of the other grants had, this one could totally revolutionise the way we worked forever. It could literally help hundreds of kids to achieve more.

As I sat at my desk a thought struck me which made me realise that I didn't need to worry. Out of all the hundreds of charities in Manchester, we had been one of the four chosen to be seen. The probability was that this was God's doing. The more I thought about it, the more I realised that I needed to be confident that His hand was on the 'N-Gage' team and all we hoped to achieve in the future. I left with my spirits soaring. God was on the case!

Fast-forwarding two weeks, it was my last day of work for 2011. I was finishing for my Christmas break. Absolutely drained and in desperate need of a holiday, I almost fell out of the office. It had been a tough few weeks with some real high points but also some huge challenges. I was wrung out. Everyone around me agreed that I needed a rest.

I stopped at reception to say goodbye to everyone and shared my joy at the thought of three whole weeks of annual leave. My gloating didn't seem to go down all that well so I walked out of the door to my car. As I got to the car I suddenly thought "Post!" I walked back into the building, smiled politely and took off my gloating 'I'm going on holiday' face.

"Sorry, did 'N-Gage' have any post?"

"Err... Nope, don't think so." said the Receptionist, checking to see.

She looked through the tray and found nothing, so I continued out of the door. We have the most annoying door in the world. When you enter you feel like it's trying to break your nose. When you leave you stand in front of it, thinking it will open automatically. But it doesn't. It always takes me about ten seconds to suss out that you have to push a button to open it. Anyway there I was trying my best to leave again and then she suddenly shouted, "Christie, you have a letter!"

I walked back in and took it, instantly realising it was important. I sat on the bench and opened it slowly. My hands were shaking. My mouth was dry and my hands were clammy and sweaty.

"Dear N-Gage…" I read,

"We are delighted to offer you the full amount..."

My heart skipped more than one beat. I turned to the Receptionist with the biggest smile and said, "I've just got a grant for £50,000!"

"Well done! Have a good break!" she replied, kindly.

I would now.

I would have a very good break indeed.

I would have the best break ever.

If God is for us, who can be against us?

Yes!

After standing at the door for the standard ten seconds, I remembered to press the button. I walked to my car feeling more than a bit shell-shocked. Sitting in the car I re-read the letter just to check I had it right. Elatedly, I rang Jo.

"You'll never guess what? We got the grant for the FULL amount!"

She was ecstatic and I could tell from the tone of her voice that, like me, she was really happy but taken aback. I then rang my Dad and he was equally chuffed. I worked my way through the staff team and trustees. I wanted everyone to share the moment with me. After all the calls and the initial flurry of excitement I knew that I needed to reserve the biggest thanks for an amazing Father who provides for His children in the most incredible and generous ways. So I prayed and thanked Him for His amazing provision.

We ran an event that Christmas, inviting some young people who had been involved in doing some Community Action projects to come and share what difference our work had made. A local police officer came and presented them all with an award. It was brilliant to see those kids rewarded for all the positive work they did with us. For many of them it would have been the first time anyone had recognised anything positive in their behaviour.

After Christmas we advertised for the Schools' Worker role and had a huge response which was really encouraging. Taking on a new person would enable me to focus on developing the charity and impacting more young people.

Building for the Future

Around this time in 2011 a local housing trust in Benchill asked for my help. They wanted me to start delivering some inclusion programmes at a youth centre they were running. They explained that they were struggling with certain young people who were acting in dangerous, anti-social and threatening ways, meaning they were constantly barred from accessing the only help in the area specifically for them. It was a frustrating picture and one that is, sadly, replicated all over the country.

The young people in question had nothing better to do than hang around outside being abusive and difficult. I put together a 6-week re-integration programme for them. The deal was that if the young people attended and improved their behaviour, they were allowed back in the centre. So I ran this for a few weeks with various groups and by and large the issues improved. Around this time the Trust were having some leadership issues and wanted a fresh pair of eyes to run the centre for a while so I was asked if we would consider taking on the management for a year.

After much discussion and prayer as a group of trustees, we decided that this was a good project to take on. Part of the deal from the Housing Trust was that they would pay 'N-Gage' £40,000 for the year. We would also have a free office for this time. We signed the deal and advertised for a Centre Manager to work for 'N-Gage' and run the centre. At the same time we relocated our offices from Didsbury to Benchill. It was a steep learning curve for me and for us all. My manager had to deal with sessional staff who were not contracted to us but to the Trust. It was a challenging time for us but helped us to see what running a youth centre entailed. We successfully got the centre back on track, hitting all the targets needed in order for it to keep its funding. At the end of the year we were able to hand over a much more stable project back to the Trust who then appointed a new manager.

CHAPTER 7

The waiting game

"And I am certain that God, who began the good work within you, will continue his work until it is finally finished on the day when Christ Jesus returns".

Philippians 1:6

Work continued to grow and develop and despite the recession we seemed to manage to expand in all the right ways at just the right time. Our daughter Amy was now five so we decided it would be good for her to have a brother or sister. We kind of assumed it would happen quickly in the same way it had when we had her. So in 2009 we started trying for another baby. Amy was deeply excited about the prospect of a new addition to the family but what followed was nearly two years of despair. Nothing happened and it was really taking its toll on us. It was really hard to stay positive for Amy when as a couple it was a really difficult time.

We prayed, we cried and we asked close friends to pray and stand with us, but as the months passed by and nothing happened it really tested my faith. I know Jo really struggled as well. It was hard to keep having to explain to Amy that we were waiting for God to make it happen and it was hard hearing her praying every night and not understanding why it was taking so long. I tried to stay strong for Jo because I could see she was really struggling. As head of the family I knew that I needed to try and keep it together where possible. But when I was alone in the car I would get frustrated and shout at God. I was perhaps at times openly cynical about where God was and what He was doing. I found it hard to keep trusting.

Amy has the impressive faith of a child and used to say to me "Don't worry Dad, a baby will come soon." but I also knew at times it was quite hard for her to stay patient when she wanted a baby sibling so badly. One day in the spring of 2011 she came to us and told us that she had been feeling sad so had gone to her room and had said to God, "Please can I have a baby brother or sister?". She distinctly heard God say a big "Yes" to her. From that moment on we decided we should change our daily prayer from "Please God, could you give us a baby?" to "Thank you God that you have promised us a baby. Please help us to be patient while we wait."

It took all our faith to believe that promise Amy had heard but we felt it was the right thing to do for her sake if nothing else.

Devastating revelation

As I said in an earlier chapter, one thing adoptive parents must wrestle with is when to share potentially horrific facts with their children.

As I was starting to think about writing this book, I spent some time at Mum and Dad's getting some facts. "How old was I when I was in the children's home?" "Where was it?" etc. etc. They filled me in with as much detail as they could so I could start to bringing my thoughts together and deciding what I would include.

In the spring of 2011 we went round to Mum and Dad's for a meal. Mum and Jo were chatting in the kitchen and Mum suddenly told her that there was something about my past that she knew she needed to share. I think she felt that, due to the nature of the information, it would be better for Jo to know it first. My poor parents had known this fact since they had had me but had never known how, or even whether to say it to me. As a parent I don't know how I would have shared something so horrible with my child, but I think Mum and Dad were right in the way they did it. If they had told me when I was younger, it would have sent me crashing even further off the rails. If they had told me at Hilltop it would have ended any chance of success I had.

When do you tell someone something devastating? There is *never* a right time.

By waiting until I was happily married with a deep faith, a loving, supportive wife and a child of my own, they sensed I was in a much better place to deal with what was coming.

When my mum had told me all those years ago about my real mum being raped there was a bit more to the story. My mum shared with Jo the horrible truth that my real mum had, in fact, been raped by her own father. I was not just the result of rape. I was also the result of incest.

As you can imagine, this took Jo some time to come to terms with.

She then had the awful job of finding the right moment to share it with me.

Again, there is never a perfect moment for such information to be shared, but as with any truth, even an especially, dark, terrifying truth, as soon as it is known and exposed it starts to be understood.

Jo and my parents were amazing as they supported me through this new hideous revelation about my past. But I didn't handle it well at all. I don't know anyone who would have.

The impact

I couldn't really get my head round it. I felt dirty and cheapened. Worse than all those years ago when Mum told me about my real mum. I had so many questions. What kind of a dad would do that to his child? As a father now it baffled my brain. As I struggled to make sense of what I knew about myself, I became incredibly depressed. We went away with some close friends a few days after Jo told me. I wanted to try to do 'normal' things... plus, I didn't want Amy to be affected by it. But, despite my best efforts, there were times when it was all too much. I just felt really tearful all the time. Indescribably deep-rooted feelings of self-loathing came to the surface. I spent about a year repeatedly saying to Jo, "Nobody likes me." I felt as though I would never recover.

My faith was really shaken and I wanted to walk away from church. I knew people were praying for me but I couldn't feel it. I felt as though no-one understood and that I couldn't be myself or tell anyone what I was going through. It was a rubbish time for us. Jo suggested I went to the GP and, eventually, I did. As I was explaining how I felt, she asked what might have triggered it. In a very quiet voice, I told her what I had found out. She looked visibly shaken as I told her. She told me that most cases like this are aborted. I was the first person she knew of who had been born as a result of that kind of rape. She put me on medication again and advised me that I needed to see a counsellor.

By now, only a couple of very close friends knew. We told them so that Jo could get some support and they could pray for us. I had been born as a result of an act of incest. I didn't know anyone in the same situation. Maybe if I could chat to someone in the same boat that would help? I 'Googled' the word, to see if any information came up but very quickly abandoned it. I wasn't ready to talk about it or even think about it. Jo was very worried about me. I wasn't sharing how I felt. I just used to go off for a drive and try and get my head around it all. I was feeling at the end of myself. I knew that I was mentally ill.

One day, when I was really low, a voice in my head said, "Drive your car fast at that big tree". I was surprised at the strength of the suggestion. It scared me. At this point I realised that I needed help and we went to see our church leaders, Anthony and Zoe. I was a right mess and could barely get my words out. They prayed for me lots and said I really needed to go and chat things through with a professional. I went and spoke to another person at church and he gave me details of a Christian counsellor. For a long time I met with him regularly.

I put these meetings in my work diary as a 'council meeting' but I think everyone knew where I was. One thing that the counsellor really worked on with me was not blaming myself for what had happened. I felt wrong and unclean and as though what had happened was my fault. I had to work through those feelings. I had also passionately hated my real mum for nearly forty years. I now had new, unfamiliar feelings for her. I began to feel immense sadness for her. She had been the victim. As I started to heal and chat it through I began to have a growing sense of admiration for her. I became sure that in any other case it would have ended with an abortion. What an amazing young girl she must have been! Mum said that she would have been in her teens when she was raped so for her to keep me was nothing short of a miracle. My real mum was a hero. She had chosen the most difficult path for herself. Part of me even started to admire her.

Over time I started to work through my complicated layered feelings and it was a very long and painful process, which I know is not totally over. After having really thought it through over time I started to have an even greater passion for my work. I wanted to make sure that my story and the horror of what I had been told could be used for good and for God. I started to know in my spirit that the legacy of that awful act had birthed something far greater than anything any of us could ever imagine. God was *for* me! If he could turn my story around there was no-one outside His reach!

The new addition

When Jo first found out the truth about my conception she confided in a close friend while she worked out if, and eventually how, to tell me. This friend knew we were trying for a baby and immediately felt there was a connection between us having another baby and me knowing the truth about my past. She believed that once my whole story was known to me God would be able to secure our future as a family. Jo didn't understand how or why this might be true but it gave her hope that there was no physical reason why Amy wouldn't have a sibling and it confirmed to her that she had to tell me what she had been told, and soon.

Incredibly, six weeks after she had told me about my conception, and almost two years after we had started trying, Jo fell pregnant. We waited until we had had the twelve week scan and then we told Amy – it felt like the longest few weeks of our lives! Jo had ordered a Babygro with the words 'I love Amy' on it. We pulled it out of the bag to show her and I have never seen Amy look so happy. Initially she seemed a bit shell-shocked but that soon turned to giddy-skipping-around joy! She was getting her long-awaited little person.

Life went on, I was still very depressed but there now seemed to be a light dawning. Ella Hope was born on the 25th of May 2012. We picked Ella because it means 'bright light'. It was the hottest day of the year and the air-con in our hospital room was broken. After the usual waiting around she made her appearance. She needed a little bit of help to get her breathing properly. I felt anxious. Births always brought back feelings of how I must have entered the world. They moved her to the other side of the room and I remember sticking to the nurse like glue as I didn't want

Ella to be separated from us for too long. She was fine. I had another baby daughter. I breathed a sigh of relief – the kind of sigh only we dads know about. I looked at Jo and Amy cuddling little Ella and for a moment I felt truly happy.

Moving forward

Work was still crazily busy. I had a contract from the police to deliver detached youth work using a youth bus that they had. We had a new Schools' Worker who I was training up after a couple of false starts with other people and Sarah Small was our Operations Manager. Rachel was now running all our community work and it was thriving and growing. My Dad was in a couple of days a week doing funding bids. We were working in six schools by now and 570 young people had been through our Schools' Work Programme. We also continued to have students coming to do placements with us. Our Board had grown and we had some new additions.

We had access to the police youth bus but I started to feel we should get our own as well. We were in the market for a truck and Sarah and I were travelling the length of the country looking at various vehicles, such as old mobile libraries, to convert. None were suitable and we were under a bit of pressure because we had put in a bid to the City Council for one.

I love how God sets things up for us as a charity! About six years earlier I had a conversation with a neighbour about my hopes and dreams for 'N-Gage'. I'd said that I'd love to get a youth bus one day. I didn't really think much more of it. All these years later at just the time we needed one, he came over and knocked on my door. He sold trucks for a living and one of his customers had just acquired about ten of them. He thought they would make great youth trucks. So we went to look at these vehicles. They were lined up in a haulage firm's yard, twenty minutes from our offices. They had been used as construction worker mobile testing centres. A Salford company had lost a contract to deliver the tests and an admin worker for the firm had bought them with a view to selling them on as horseboxes. We picked the best one. It was a 2005 registration plate 7.5ton truck. It would have cost £100,000 new. The lady selling them only wanted £6,500! So we bought one and my friend Joe Monck converted it so we could use it as a mobile youth centre.

My friend Simon Chesterson helped as well, removing the old vehicle graphics and putting in audio visual gear. It was a massive learning curve for us and had to be done on a tight budget but we did it! I think it is the one thing professionally that I am most proud of achieving. It has been used by hundreds of young people, helping them to be heard and valued. It has been a way for us to show God's love to so many forgotten youth on tough estates and, like all of our work, has been proven to reduce anti-social behaviour and crime.

Time for a rest

By now were running an annual team day away. So in December 2012 we took the whole team away for the day to Lymm Baptist Church. It was time to do some 'bigger picture' thinking, to pray and review what we had done, and more importantly, what God had achieved over the past twelve months. Following this day I was going to be taking 3 months off. Due to my depression and the exhaustion of having worked solidly for nearly a decade setting up and developing 'N-Gage', the trustees agreed that it would be a good idea for me to take a sabbatical.

I finished work in December 2012 and would not be back in work until April 2013. That would be hard for me! By my own admission I am a workaholic. Even in 'down time' I'm thinking about work. For the last seven years I had been constantly eating, sleeping and working on 'N-Gage'. A lot of what happened for 'N-Gage' happened because it was me that made it happen, so it would be interesting to walk away for a while. The trustees stepped up to the plate. It was left to Sarah, Rachel and my dad to run the ship while I was away. I don't think it was always easy for them, but they did a sterling job of keeping things running.

The only real condition to my time off was that I had to stay motivated, find things to do and keep active. In the January we took a holiday to Dorset. As it was out of season we got a massive house with sea views very cheaply. Ella was just starting to be mobile and Amy was excited to get a week out of school. We went to my favourite place in the whole country. Durdle

Door is an amazing cove on the Dorset coast. It brought back memories of when we had been there on day trips on Crusader holidays before I became a teenager. The colours were brilliant and even in the winter it looked great. Amy and I walked down the steep path. I could see she was impressed with the view. It felt good to stop and breathe again.

Rehabs and recommitments

As part of my time off work, I planned a trip to Harvey, Illinois, near Chicago in March 2013. My friend from church, Lynn Swart, knew some guys out there and she suggested it would be good for me to spend some time with them. I packed up my cases with some trepidation. I was a depressed man feeling tired and alone. I arrived at Manchester Airport and went to check my case in, which I had borrowed from a friend. The lady said, "Is this your bag?" Not being hugely well travelled and a bit dizzy I said "No" because strictly speaking it wasn't! It didn't go down that well. She radioed for a colleague as I was asked to stand to one side. I was allowed through only after a minute and thorough search of all my possessions. I could see people sniggering at me.

I arrived in Chicago to be met by 'The Doc' and one of his colleagues. I was taken to a centre they ran. Lynn had explained a bit about what they did but nothing could prepare me for the next ten days. Bearing in mind I was still depressed, not great at travelling and a long way from my wife and kids. I had no idea what to expect. We drove from the airport for about forty minutes to a suburb of Chicago. Two men called John Sullivan and Ray C Banks had come to collect me (I love the fact that people in the US want to tell you their middle name initial, but keep you guessing about their whole name).

Restoration Ministries does lots of life changing work. They have houses for addicts to come and live in and get clean. They run thrift stores, boxing clubs for young people, a youth centre, bible classes, church, outreach to the homeless in downtown Chicago, plus lots more. John was a force of nature and his passion and drive left me utterly exhausted. He had been a high-flying dentist but, in response to the need he saw in his city, had set up loads of ministries instead. I was in awe of him and the work he and the team did.

Each week they drove to a drug treatment centre called Branden House.

This was my first off-site visit. I walked into the rehab and felt instantly fearful. I stuck close to the people who brought me and sat down hoping to somehow blend my black face into the white walls. There were all sorts of characters filtering in. Ex-gangsters, drug addicts, alcoholics, you name it, they were there. They were coming in to have a Bible study. One guy had a teardrop tattoo under his eye. I scanned my memory thinking, "What does that mean? What does that mean?" A few minutes later the penny dropped as I remembered it was a gang sign that you had murdered someone. I shuddered and tried to stay as still as possible.

Barbara, the Doc's wife, stood up holding her bible and proceeded to talk. As she spoke, a respectful hush fell on the room and as she led the meeting, hardened, hurt men kept putting their hands up.

"Pastor Barbara can I be free from sin?"

"Yes." she said gently.

Another person would agree and say, "Yes, you can. Jesus has saved my life."

They were all agreeing with her words and saying "Amen" as she spoke. It was a powerful and moving experience. She introduced me to the group and a guy latched on to me because he was called Chris. We chatted for a while and he explained how he had got into drugs and that it had ruined his life. He was now trying to get clean and live for Jesus. I went back to the place I was staying and prayed. I wanted God to continue to heal me and make me better. I had a strange sense of hope in the midst of my dark depression that Jesus would help pull me through. Why was He letting me see this if not to show me that His hand was on my life too?

The week continued in much the same vein. I visited a couple of high schools. I was struck by how multi-cultural they were, but also by how each community seemed to be unintentionally segregated. Black in one corner, Hispanics in another etc. I was told it was a melting pot that frequently flared up. In one school they were mourning a girl who had been caught in crossfire outside as a gang battle raged. She had been fatally shot and the memory of her death was raw in the faces of all I saw.

All week I was told they were taking me Downtown. In my ignorance I assumed this was a nice place and a treat. It was actually the underground roads under the city centre. It was not a place anyone would choose to go. We filled the van with sandwiches and water. It was freezing cold and it had snowed the night before. We drove through the city centre. I was amazed by how big every building was – it was just like the movies.

We drove down into the underground area of the city and parked up. The icy cold wind blasted my face. We walked for a little while until we arrived at the most pitiful gathering of homeless people I have ever seen. By the side of the road were barriers a bit higher than my waist. I peered over one. What I saw was like a little village. This was not tents though. It was people in sleeping bags covered in cardboard boxes. Basically anything they could find so that they could be sheltered. There were lots and lots of these little 'communities' on every available bit of the unused road. Our job was to hand out sandwiches and water. I suddenly felt so useless and emotional. I was surrounded by a team of people who had experienced what these homeless people were experiencing. They knew firsthand how hard their lives were. The Doc and Barbara had taken them off the street, rescued them, given them a home and enabled them to get clean, and then had allowed them to come back and help others in the same situation. It was amazing to watch. UNBELIEVABLE.

We moved from place to place, handing out water. I felt more and more emotional and was fighting having a very big cry. A girl sat next to me and whispered,

"I was like them a few months ago and look at what Jesus has done for me! He saved my life!"

As I saw a tear trickle down her cheek, that was me gone! My own tears started to flow. I couldn't control them and nor did I want to. It felt right and appropriate to cry. So I sat there and bawled for a while. I wasn't really bothered who saw. I was mentally low and away from home but that wasn't the source of my tears. God was on my case big time. We got out and gave another 'body' in a mangy sleeping bag a sandwich and some water. He explained he had some health issues that didn't sound too good. Someone said, "Can we pray for you?"

So we did.

I was surprised to be asked to pray too. I had NO idea what to say. I was just silly, useless, depressed Christie from Manchester. I prayed as best as I could, and then got back in the van. I was very moved. I felt God saying, "If I need to take you to the lowest parts of society and show you the worst of the world to show you how to live for me, I will."

I sat in the back of the van and recommitted my life to Jesus. This had to be a new start for me. I vowed I would try and live my life for Jesus again when I got back. For the first time in months I felt close to God. I called Jo and told her what had happened and she was thrilled.

Coming in to land

I returned to Manchester and did a leadership course with the National Council of Voluntary Organisations. It was a great way to ease back into work. The team at 'N-Gage' were glad to have me back. I felt different and was able to start work again with a fresh perspective.

What followed was the maddest period of challenge and change for us as we coped with various key staff changes. I sensed that if I wasn't careful I would undo all the benefits of my sabbatical. My Board and I managed to work through it but it was a tough time.

Meeting Carl again

In 2014 I was asked to speak about 'N-Gage' at one of the Grow Groups (small midweek groups) from our church. As I was leaving I noticed a man washing his car as I got into mine. He looked up and said "Hello" and I recognised him as Carl, my old tutor from catering college. I went over to say hello. He remembered me and we got chatting. He explained how tough it had been for him when he started at the college as the only black lecturer. His passion for learning was still evident. He told me that some of the other lads who had done the course had taken different paths; some into drugs etc. and some had sadly now passed away. He told me he was now 80 years old, that he was very proud of me and that I should continue to chase my dreams. It was the most unbelievable chat I had had in a long time. His wife arrived home and she stood talking with us as well. I could tell from my brief time with her that she was an incredibly wise lady. This little meeting I had was a God moment. I felt at the time that I needed a bit of encouragement because running something like 'N-Gage' can sometimes make you feel insecure. Here was a man who had inspired me and helped to instil a work ethic in me, at a time when I had none, challenging me to carry on and heaping praise on me with no idea how much it would bless me. I left after half an hour or so and went home to tell Jo what had happened. I promised Carl as I left that I would post a copy of this book through his door when it was done.

A bright future

Today 'N-Gage' continues to grow as God keeps us trusting in Him and pulling together. The vision remains to 'help young people unlock their full potential' and we are managing to do that in so many ways that I could never have dreamed of. We are looking at a Community Asset Transfer which will involve taking an old youth centre from Manchester City Council and turning it into our first N-Gage youth centre.

We have been successful in our bids to expand our detached work and acquire another vehicle. We are looking at what an N-Gage school might look like. We are constantly striving to improve the service we offer and reach more young people. By the time you are reading this book we hope all this will have happened – and we are daring to believe God for even more.

I never forget when I look at a young person who we work with that I was like them not so long ago. I was disaffected, angry, frustrated and misunderstood. I know what it is like to be alone, distrusted, discarded and labelled as a 'problem'.

God has been so kind to me. He has, like Doc and Barbara in Chicago, rescued me from a makeshift village of misfits where I did not want to live. He has taken me away from a life of crime, temptation, fear and resentment. He has made me confront the worst of my past to get to the best of my future. I know that the legacy of N-Gage will live on in countless lives and I am grateful that every time I failed, God picked me up and helped me start again.

Moving forward

I don't know you or what you have had to overcome in your life. I don't know what you have suffered or what you have had to endure. As you look back, try and see what God has taught you, what He has shown you and who He has put in your path. Be grateful for who you are and what you have become. Keep dreaming for what is ahead.

I came across this amazing prayer recently that I say over you and over myself. Determine with me today not to let your past hold you back from the things God has planned for you.

"Dear God,

Please take away my pain and despair of yesterday and any unpleasant memories and replace them with your glorious promise of new hope. Show me a fresh Holy Spirit-inspired way of relating to negative things that have happened. I ask you for the mind of Christ so I can discern your voice from the voice of my past. I pray that former rejection and deep hurts will not colour what I see and hear now.

Help me to see all the choices I have ahead of me that can alter the direction of my life. I ask you to empower me to let go of the painful events and heartaches that would keep me bound. Thank You for Your forgiveness that you have offered to me at such a great price. Pour it into my heart so I can relinquish bitterness hurts and disappointments that have no place in my life. Please set me free to forgive those who have sinned against me and caused me pain and also myself. Open my heart to receive your complete forgiveness and amazing grace. You have promised to bind up my wounds (Psalm 147:3) and restore my soul (Psalm 23:3)"

Sue Augustine, *When Your Past Is Hurting Your Present*

Epilogue

I thought the book was finished and then the following happened which I just had to include. People who know me well will know that I am a complete petrol head. I have loved cars my whole life and am a total geek when it comes to car facts.

A couple of months ago I said to Jo jokingly "I wish I'd got a BMW 3 Series Estate". The reason I said this was that my current car, a leased VW CC, was lovely but on occasions I struggle with my back and it was not always easy getting in it as it was a coupe style car.

Jo said, "Why don't you ring up the finance company and see how much it would be to swap or hand it back?"

So I did. VW finance gave me a couple of options but both were too expensive and required us to have a lump sum of cash, so we decided to plod on with the CC and I didn't really think any more of it.

A few days later I was working at my desk when I got a phone call. Someone had been given my details from one of our supporters. Was I looking for a car? I chatted to this person and they explained that they had a BMW 520d. They were looking to give it away to someone who was involved in charity work as they felt that was what God was telling them to do! I went home and chatted to Jo and we decided to find out more. A few days later I met the person at a coffee shop. We chatted about the work I do then they showed me the car. It was a top spec 5 Series. I took it for a spin around the block and loved it. A few days later the car was handed to me along with enough money to clear the finance on my VW, releasing us from significant regular costs. How amazing that God should choose to bless our family in this way!

Support the work of N-Gage

I want to invite you to do something about what you have read. Perhaps you could join us in praying for our work. We need people to get on their knees for us in everything we are involved in. Maybe you are someone who could get involved with one of our projects or volunteer for us in some capacity? Perhaps you know a young person or group of young people who are troubled and have lost their way.

Finally can I ask you to consider partnering with me? When I was conceived it was through a negative act, but when I was allowed to be born. God had a plan for my life. Many young people hit our streets every evening with nothing to do other than feel as though no-one wants them. I want to show them that if God can turn my life around so dramatically, there is hope for them too. Will you help me do that? Will you give regularly to our work in order that we might take on more staff, reach out to more young people and change the world where we live?

Each person on earth has the potential for an amazing future but they may have an awful past and a troubled present. I can't turn back the clock for them, but I can give them hope and help them find a God who can show them that their best is yet to come. Will you join me?

If you feel you can help then please get in touch using the tear off slip on the next page and let us know how you can support our work. One of the things I have felt over the years is that sharing my story is powerful. If you feel you would like to book me to come and speak at your church or an event please contact us. I have had a challenging life but am pleased to be able to testify about all the amazing things God has done for me. The expectation was that I would get angry when I was younger and end up doing something that would land me in prison. I was certainly on that path but God had a much bigger and better plan for me.

 **Supporting N-Gage**

Please return this form to:
N-Gage, Benchill Community Centre, Benchill Road,
Wythenshawe, Manchester M22 8EJ

N-Gage is passionate about enabling young people to reach their full potential. Our innovative programmes are having a massive impact on the young people we work with and we are largely dependent on the generosity of people like you.

Thank you for your support.

Name:
Address:

Account Name: N-Gage
Bank Details: Barclays Bank, Didsbury branch.

Account Number: 90647233

Sort Code: 20-26-20

Telephone Number:
Email:

- I enclose a cheque made payable to *N-Gage* for the sum of £_____

- I have made a donation of £_____ direct into N-Gage's bank account (see box for bank account details)

- I have set up a standing order for £_____a month to N-Gage's bank account.

- I would like to Gift Aid this donation and all future donations until I notify otherwise.

Signature:

Date: /   /

giftaid it

To qualify for Gift Aid, you must pay an amount of UK Income Tax and/or Capital Gains Tax at least equal to the tax that the charity reclaims on your donations in the appropriate tax year. Tax year is 6

For more information visit www.n-gage.org.uk or email admin@n-gage.org.uk
Charity number: 1117843. Company number: 9210663

1. ☐ I would like to book Christie Spurling to speak at our event.
2. ☐ I would like to order/display copies of this book.
3. ☐ I would like to book an N-Gage youth work programme.
4. ☐ I would like to explore Ivy Church Manchester.
5. ☐ I would like to book the N-Gage Truck for an event.
6. ☐ I would like to explore partnering with N-Gage.
7. ☐ I would like to go on an Alpha course. Please send me more details.

For more information or to speak to us about any of the above please contact the N-Gage office by emailing admin@n-gage.org.uk or calling 0161 637 1302.